Managing Through Turbulent Times

The 7 rules of crisis management

by Anthony Holmes

HARRIMAN HOUSE LTD

3A Penns Road
Petersfield
Hampshire
GU32 2EW
GREAT BRITAIN

Tel: +44 (0)1730 233870
Fax: +44 (0)1730 233880
Email: enquiries@harriman-house.com
Website: www.harriman-house.com

First published in Great Britain in 2009

The right of Anthony Holmes to be identified as the author has been asserted
in accordance with the Copyright, Design and Patents Act 1988.

978-1-906659-11-0

British Library Cataloguing in Publication Data
A CIP catalogue record for this book can be obtained from the British Library.

Printed and bound by the CPI Group, Antony Rowe.

For my daughter Kate

Contents

Preface

As I write this book in the final quarter of 2008 the world appears to have moved to the edge of the precipice of the worst economic dislocation since the great depression that began in 1929.

The causes have been argued over ceaselessly in the media, and politicians are beginning to pander to a general desire to accuse and punish those who can be held responsible.

In 2007 few so-called experts and commentators predicted the events that occurred during 2008 or that the world economy would be in this parlous situation but, nonetheless, here we are.

It is interesting how critically important medium-term international problems that topped the agenda at the beginning of 2008 have now been subordinated.

Nothing has occurred to reduce the threats of international terrorism and climate change but their prominence has diminished. It is as though there is a limit to the number of society changing events we are able to handle simultaneously. It seems that international terrorism and climate change must wait until we can reposition them in the socio-political landscape that will follow the current economic turbulence and the financial resources devoted to them are constrained until, once again, we can afford them!

To take a specific example; the US and British governments are moving towards the withdrawal of their military presence from Iraq. Has the task they set themselves been completed and the objectives achieved? Is it just that the mandate that legitimised the US and UK presence expired on 31st December 2008? Or has the cost of this entanglement simply become unjustifiable in the situation that now prevails?

And what of climate change?

Well you can probably hear the voices of those arguing that our reaction can wait for a couple years, can't it?

In the face of economic Armageddon everything else is pushed from prominence. Priorities are fragile and mutable. They tend to be dominated not by the events we forecast but by those we fail to predict. Darfor, Zimbabwe, Democratic Republic of the Congo, Iraq, Afghanistan, Mumbai, the Chinese Olympics; in years to come 2008 will be notable for none of these.

We might say that these are examples of politicians practicing management in turbulent times. The political horizon of expectation shrinks to the duration of the recession, military entanglements and capital expenditures fall victim to cost reduction programmes, tax revenues decrease and borrowing increases. Re-election becomes dependent on how the electorate perceives a politician to have confronted the fire that is now at everyone's feet.

Having worked through the recessions of the early 1980s and 1990s I do not find this to be unusual. In fact, institutional failure to predict the onset of a cyclical downturn or the bursting of an asset price bubble is as predictable as the media and governments turning to the premature recognition of the green shoots of economic recovery when gloom and disaster is all around.

Despite increasingly complex econometric models no one really knows what will happen other than the descent into recession is inevitable. How deep it will be and how long it will last are effectively unknowable. So those who call the bottom of the trend line and the onset of economic spring are false prophets, as were those who denied the possibility of the position we now occupy.

What can be said is that 2009 and 2010 will be turbulent. There will be false dawns. Big companies will collapse. (In 2007, who, for example, would have believed a prediction that Lehman Brothers would file for bankruptcy in 2008?) Many innocent, diligent, wage earning people's lives will be damaged. Politicians and managers will be discredited, optimism will be sought and the managed world will seek leadership.

I believe that there is an important distinction between management and leadership. But, in this book, I do not want to confuse the theme by dwelling too much on the difference.

I think, however, that it is worthwhile declaring that I believe the capacity for effective leadership to be a rare attribute that cannot be realised by an individual simply because they happen to occupy a position of responsibility at a moment when circumstances demand a leader rather than a manager.

If leadership is an attribute present in a person, then a change in the prevailing situation to something turbulent will usually allow it to emerge. If no-one with leadership capabilities is available then managers remain responsible for dealing with the turbulence their organisation encounters, and trying to imitate the characteristics of past leaders while practicing the same managerial conduct is an inappropriate response.

In turbulent times artificial turning points assume an irrational significance. The turn of the year from 2008 (the year of dislocation) to 2009 (the year of hope), the inauguration of Barack Obama as President of the USA in January 2009, the northern hemisphere spring and the renewal it signified all added something expectant to the general sentiment.

But before any of this hope can become reality we must endure a bleak midwinter of economic discontent. This is a great turbulence, the like of which few have experienced and in which many people in positions of authority have little idea of how to act. This is a bad time for an individual with responsibility for the wellbeing of others to be at the bottom of the learning curve.

However, let me sound an optimistic note. Most companies will survive, economic growth will resume, some of the corporate sick will be healed.

There are positive actions that managers can take. They are rarely taught in business school and tend to fade from the managerial memory as the previous recession recedes.

I hope this book will remind some of you of some of these lost notions and that other readers will find renewed confidence from the knowledge that guidance is available.

Anthony Holmes

London, December 2008

About the author

Anthony Holmes is an international corporate turnaround specialist and transitional leadership expert who has led the revival of 7 companies over 15 years, in industries as diverse as utilities, construction, consumer durables and telecoms.

His 30-year international business career spans strategic consultancy, investment banking and senior corporate management. Anthony lives in London and holds a BA in Economics from Sheffield University and an MSc in Political Theory from the London School of Economics.

Acknowledgements

I would like to thank the following people who have helped me to shape the ideas and who have read, commented on and edited this manuscript:

Michael J Arnold, Richard Ball, Col. (Rtrd) Jonathan Frere MBE, Prof. Janet Coleman, Zena James, David Jephson, W.D. McClelland, David Peters and Ray Pollard.

Suzanne Anderson of Harriman House who undertook the onerous task of editing my original draft and then suffered the irritation of my late additions. Francesca Warren who provided invaluable guidance, and the indomitable Mrs B (really Jo Clear) who tolerated my eccentricity.

Of course any errors and omissions are entirely my responsibility.

Introduction

Turbulent times are pernicious. They are the periods when the structural and financial weaknesses of our organisations become exposed and consequently, because of the stress they induce, some, perhaps many, of the individuals we rely on to manage our institutions begin to function ineffectively and sometimes irrationally.

Our language expresses our conceptual preferences and few people enjoy or want to preserve a period of turbulence. We speak about 're-establishing control' and never about 'recreating turbulence'. We prefer peace to war; certainty to uncertainty; calm to storm; progress to retreat; compliance to lawlessness; positive to negative.

In general, our social system has developed to function best in times of stability, when a significant level of control is possible, the rule of law prevails and reliable predictions of future conditions are feasible.

So turbulence is an abnormal and undesirable state in which normal procedures are unreliable or simply ineffective and we want to navigate through the abnormality quickly and safely in order to resume our day to day activity in a more conducive environment.

Natural disasters such as the Asian Tsunami of 2004 and Hurricane Katrina that devastated New Orleans in 2005 provide examples of events that have a significant impact and occur suddenly without adequate warning to facilitate protective or preventative action. The only response is to address the consequences.

Economic turbulence is different in that it emerges gradually, is sometimes predicted, always argued about in advance of its impact, often denied and occasionally ignored. Despite any advance discussions most managers are unprepared. Turbulent times, irrespective of the cause, are anathema to corporate managers. Turmoil undermines the conditions they prefer, some say need, to ply their profession.

Moreover, economic turbulence in the form of recession is a natural feature of the business cycle that is characteristic of the capitalist system and it is therefore an ever-present possibility. It is a necessary adjustment phase that releases excess pressure from the system created when asset values exceed their economic value by too great an amount. In simple terms when a bubble forms.

So why are managers anxious about operating in what should be an anticipated phase that has been encountered sufficiently often to have enabled the learnings to be codified in the managerial toolkit?

I believe that such general economic turbulence is not dissimilar to widespread warfare. You cannot avoid it, you may or may not survive or be disabled, you may endure without physical damage and, for a minority, it will be the most rewarding period you have encountered, but few of those affected by it make adequate preparations.

When hostilities have ceased most people do not want to pour over the ashes but to get on with rebuilding, so the lessons are rarely learned and each subsequent occurrence is confronted without preparation as if it were a novel event.

My objective is not to take political turbulence and apply it to the corporate world, although the similarities will resonate throughout what I have to say. My concern is exclusively with how corporate managers approach turbulence and I shall be inclined towards how they should act in a climate of general economic turbulence, although this isn't the only type of disorder that can affect their business.

Turbulence arises in companies because:

- Companies and markets do not have the dependable nature of a machine that enables them to be controlled in all situations.

- The economic world is not a knowable and controllable place although we would like it be so and, for most of the time as managers, we delude ourselves that it is, more or less.

- Over the last 50 years it has become clear to mathematicians and economists that the more interlinked a system is the more it is susceptible to chaotic episodes and turbulence.

- Additionally, it is apparent that the faster you run a system and therefore approach its operating limit the more unstable it becomes.

There are three big ideas which I believe provide the greatest influence:

- The advent of modern telecoms and computers has facilitated an exponential rise in both connectivity and networking, which has removed the limits to the pace of activities previously imposed by the speed of communication.

- We have the capability to delude ourselves that more sophisticated analytical tools and models enable us to accelerate our activity securely to a hyper pace and thereby engage in marginal activities or operate at a scale that previously was untenable.

- We can fund this by increased leverage which removes the constraint of capital availability but increases the company's vulnerability to financial distress.

As managers we seek the comfort of stability and control but perceive (and then deny) actual and potential instability, but there are situations the reality of which we cannot ignore and we argue that we cannot act because these are chaotic situations of complexity and are unresponsive to our conventional toolkit.

Most of our scientific management tools were not designed to function in a period of instability or economic contraction. They originated in an age when our economic system was less interconnected and somewhat slower paced. It is not surprising, therefore, that they do not seem to work as well today as they have in the past.

The near collapse of the world's financial system in 2008, which is the most interconnected and model-driven sector, and the catastrophic pace at which it disintegrated, illustrates the dangers.

Through trial and error we may, eventually and retrospectively, formulate new tools and procedures but in doing so we need not begin at the point of ignorance and inexperience at the bottom of the learning curve.

Nor can we rely on economic downturns and corporate distress being self-correcting. They do not represent a pause in an inevitable long-term stable trend of growth and profitable development. They precipitate the collapse and elimination of units of economic activity, especially those that are vulnerable because they have reached the final phase of their lifespan. In the same way that a pernicious virus takes the lives of the weakest, the very young and the old and infirm, so the turbulence of an economic downturn destroys vulnerable companies and leaves others disabled.

What shall we do as managers operating in unstable times, when the reassurance we desire is absent and the uncertainty of today promises an unpredictable tomorrow?

We must identify the nature of the areas and the times of instability and embrace uncertainty. We must rediscover and apply different, sometimes counter-intuitive and unconventional, methodologies which have been honed in recessions and other turbulent situations but which are discarded and forgotten when the cyclical economic winter turns to spring.

That is what this book is about.

1

What do I mean by turbulence?

What I have in mind when I discuss turbulence is a state of disorder characterised by confusion resulting from unexpected deviation or agitation. What has been called a period of permanent white water.

Turbulence arises when the reliability of our understanding of cause and effect weakens and breaks, and uncertainty grows. Effects arise unexpectedly because their causes are either obscure or are ignored. Additionally, the frequency and magnitude of these unanticipated events increases.

In chapter 4 I use this scale of certainty from conviction to doubt as one axis of a turbulence matrix that helps to visualise an organisation's relative position by considering the degree of internal harmony and the degree of confidence management has in its understanding of external events.

Turbulence can also be characterised as degrees of unstable complexity. Think about it in terms of an equation. Our social and economic systems are extremely complex and an equation that models them, were it possible to do so without substantial simplification, would be large and enormously intricate with many variables. If only a few of these variables change rapidly and continuously the equation may not yield a stable solution and the output will appear turbulent.

Although we tend to regard turbulence as being an abnormal condition it is, in reality, the default state. It is order that is unnatural. If left unmanaged all organised things appear to revert to a state of disorder[1] and nothing known to the physical sciences arises spontaneously from disorder into some complex functional form.

---

[1] For those of a scientific mind the second law of thermodynamics proves this for physical objects and I contend that social systems such as companies and states show a similar tendency towards increasing entropy.

However, biological and social systems seem different. They appear to evolve from simple beginnings into very complex structures. The paradox is that while the system as a whole appears to follow a path of self-organisation in the direction of increasing complexity, the substructures and individual units within them follow the path of change from order to disorder.

While unfolding of history may, from a distance, appear to be a persistent trend of progress towards greater complexity, closer examination reveals that it is punctuated by turbulent accelerations and reversals. States and empires emerge, grow, decline and collapse as do technologies, institutions and companies.

Stability is seemingly the special case state in which the decay of one component is balanced by the emergence of another. Turbulent change occurs only when the direction of change of a majority of components becomes similar.

Control through management activity is directed at both the system level, through government and regulatory intervention, and at the substructure level of individual constituent institutions. But there are times when the macro conditions are shaped in such a way that they compel many of the constituent institutions to adopt parallel trajectories that point to either boom or bust and lead to the unintended volatile change we experience as turbulence.

These forces are transmitted through the behaviour of people acting as social beings. But our natural state is not to live in such complex highly structured groups serviced by equally complicated contrived support systems. It is claimed by some that our 'state of nature'[2] is disordered, competitive, aggressive and bloody and that it is probably the change

---

[2] See Thomas Hobbes, *Leviathan.*

to living in small tribal groups that offered sufficient security and division of labour to ensure a life above that of subsistence. But the stability of these coalitions appears to become less reliable as their membership increases.

Today, in the developed economies, we regard even such subsistence conditions of life to be barbaric and, if we are forced to imagine what life would be like in such a world, we recoil with fear and horror. We have become used to the benefits that appear to be a dividend of our progressively more complex society.

But, like technology, our economic systems are artificial. The significant difference being that, unlike technology, they were not designed from first principles but are emergent, often in unpredictable ways, and periodically they evolve into a situation that proves to be unsustainable. A so-called bifurcation point.

It is never possible to retrace the path that led to this tipping point and return to the stability of the preceding period. The Greek philosopher Heraclitus[3] explained it succinctly by stating:

"You could not step twice into the same river; for other waters are ever flowing on to you."[4]

Adjustments in our economic system occur naturally, albeit suddenly, as the established certainties dissolve to bring turmoil when the system flips from progress to regress. The rate of change within the system accelerates and the turbulence that arises when the system approaches its maximum operating level brings instability as regular control processes, on which we have come to rely, become less effective.

---

[3] Heraclitus; circa 544-483 BCE.

[4] Heraclitus, *On the Universe.*

Faced with an uncomfortably rapid rate of change, management usually attempts to respond by speeding up their analysis and decision-making processes. But this can lead to information overload. To keep pace, as more data is demanded, the information gathered must be processed faster than existing systems, including our brains, have been designed to operate and therefore, as time is of the essence, analysis is undertaken either partially or badly or both.

The result is a slowing of the process of rational decision-making at the moment it needs to accelerate. To compensate estimate, guess and intuition may feature more dominantly leading to poor decisions taken under pressure and implemented without conviction.

Turbulence can arise in several ways. It may be felt generally or it may just affect a single company. Some of the more obvious causes of turbulence are:

- (i) General economic turbulence resulting from the formation and dramatic ending of a bubble of inflated asset prices in one major segment of the economy.

  (ii) A recession, when many sectors of a national economy or several linked economies regress simultaneously.

- Some unexpected external event such as war, revolution, a terrorist attack, a natural disaster or a dramatic increase in the price of a strategic commodity such as oil.

  Wars tend to create disorder for longer periods than terrorist attacks. The latter impose significant changes on behaviour but it is interesting how quickly the community adapts.

  Similarly, natural disasters, such as the Asian Tsunami of 2004, have an immediate and massively negative impact that increases with proximity but, while creating great loss of life and physical damage, they tend not to lead to substantial structural changes at the macro level. The world that emerges from the rebuild is recognisable as similar to that which preceded the event.

The oil price shock of 1973 is a good case history of the turmoil that can follow the unexpected increase in the price of a key commodity. The world adjusted to the new cost level but the transition to a new point of stability was neither rapid nor comfortable.

- Economic turbulence can be sector specific. But if the sector is substantial or significantly interconnected with the rest of the economy, as in the case of oil in 1973, then the turmoil can rapidly migrate as the shock waves radiate outwards.

Arguably the best example is the near collapse of the world banking system in 2008. Imprudent risk management by some financial institutions created an unstable bubble in the price of US real estate, which imploded leading to the virtual cessation of global interbank lending, the collapse of banks due to illiquidity and the stalling of capital flows on which the world economy relies.

- Other causes of turbulence are organisation specific. Examples are product recalls (thalidomide), substantial class actions (the tobacco and asbestos industries are notable examples), enduring industrial disputes (Skychefs), plant closures or failures (Union Carbide at Bophal), and liquidity problems (Enron, Long-Term Capital Management).

A far as the general economy is concerned each of these cases represents a single, easily identifiable problem on which resources can be focussed. To simplify, for the economy as a whole it is an equation with one variable.

- Organisations move through a lifespan (which I discuss at length in chapter 3). At certain points the nature of their business must change. For example, the phase of infancy characterised by lack of scale progresses to growth, during which the business expands at a rate that cannot be supported by the systems and assets employed previously. The change from infancy to growth is turbulent because it requires the rapid abandonment of the procedures on which the business has relied and the risky acquisition of systems that are unfamiliar in anticipation of a future scale that remains uncertain.

  At a later point in its lifespan the organisation drifts from maturity into decline, bringing a different but equally survival-threatening form of turbulence.

As the title suggests, in this book I concentrate on turbulence in the general economy (turbulent times) and comment on turbulence that is organisation specific only in passing.

For many obvious reasons we do not welcome, but seek to avoid, a phase in which our social stability diminishes and so we recognise a common interest in taking whatever action is necessary to restore stability as quickly as possible.

To some extent it matters little how or why this disorder arises. The important consideration is that it is a fact of life that cannot be ignored if stability is to be restored.

Is turbulence a bad thing?

The answer is; not necessarily so if it endures over the very short run. It is a seemingly unavoidable component of change without which there can be no progress.

So, if we want progress we must accept the end of the status quo and migration to something new. All journeys involve some disruption and the acceptance of greater risk.

However, if the turbulence is unexpected or of a magnitude or duration that undermines stability in fundamental ways then it is not regarded as progressive but as disruptive and potentially destructive to important elements of the established infrastructure.

Thus, if turbulence cannot be avoided, there is a general desire to contain it to a short and infrequent period, the onset of which is predictable.

You might imagine significant economic turbulence as a plague-like disease that infects the population. Irrespective of the social impact the consequence for the individual patient is debilitating, may be life-threatening and certainly requires treatment.

It is the degree of turbulence that determines whether it is a bad thing.

What do we want to accomplish from management activity in turbulent times?

Primarily we want to re-establish stability or at least to reduce the turmoil to a bearable level. But what, in the corporate arena, is a bearable level? It is the level at which the potential changes are unlikely to cause the business to collapse in the short to medium term. What this level is will differ from company to company and from country to country.

The most useful analogy is of an earthquake. Geophysical turbulence occurs all the time and most buildings cope with this background level. But there is a magnitude at which some buildings will collapse whereas others, that are more 'flexible', will survive in good shape. The greater the magnitude of the quake and the longer it endures, the fewer the buildings that are going to withstand the turbulence. Each building will have a unique threshold of maximum endurance at which its collapse will not be gradual but will probably be catastrophic.

As with buildings and earthquakes, so with companies.

Markets are never calm but the background turbulence is bearable. Indeed, our economic system would cease to function without fluctuations in price and supply as there would be no markets. Each company has a different tolerance to turbulence and although similar structures have been tested to destruction in previous unstable episodes, the lessons provided are often forgotten when designing new corporate structures.

We must also bear in mind that our social and economic systems have evolved to adapt only to a relatively slow rate of change and we call this progress, believe it to be necessary and design organisations, systems and protocols to manage this moderate change that we have come to regard as a stable condition.

Previous generations would regard our 'stable' rate of change as extremely turbulent and so it is clear that, given sufficient time, we adapt to become tolerant of a degree of turbulence that we once regarded as unbearable.

We are not equipped socially, technically or psychologically to live comfortably with turmoil significantly above our background level, so we are impelled to act in order to return our social and economic activity to comparative stability.

It is our inability to adapt quickly, magnified by institutional and contractual inflexibility, that makes these significant deviations from expected trends so threatening.

We also find it difficult to abandon the protocols that have served us well at the background level of turbulence and on which we have come to depend, and therefore tend to hold onto them until substantial change becomes not just desirable but irresistible.

For example, our objective is always to end wars and revolutions in order to terminate the social disruption that they cause. Similarly, we want to terminate economic turmoil as quickly as possible to minimise the risk that it may damage our financial wellbeing. We want to re-establish stability (the background level of turbulence) because we see this as a prerequisite for making orderly progress towards desirable social and financial goals.

We want to make progress because equilibrium is never more than a fragile, transitory state and moving forward is preferable to regression. Progress may be the raison d'être of the manager but moderating the rate of progress is necessary to feel in control.

2

What are the limits to management?

In this chapter I want to consider the role of management. In chapter 3 I discuss how the practice of management alters throughout the corporate lifespan, and in chapter 4 how the psychology of managers changes as economic conditions deteriorate and the stability of their company is jeopardised.

The late Peter Drucker[5] has been called the most influential management thinker of modern times. His 1954 book entitled *The Practice of Management* was a seminal work which described what has become known as management theory.

According to Drucker it is the application of management that makes resources productive. Not capital. Not labour. But management.

He also said that the management function embraces certain basic beliefs of modern Western society, in particular the belief that it is possible to control man's livelihood through the systematic organisation of economic resources.

John Kotter[6] states that the role of the manager is to perform the following four functions:

Planning	The science of logically deducing the means to achieve given ends.
Budgeting	Reducing plans to financial programmes.
Organising	Creating an organisational structure to facilitate the accomplishment of the plans.
Controlling	Monitoring progress to identify deviations from the plans and budgets, and implementing actions to rectify any adverse variance.

---

[5] Peter F. Drucker (1909-2005); *Professor of Social Science and Management at Claremont Graduate University in Claremont, California.*

[6] Prof. John P. Kotter (b.1947); Harvard Business School.

This summarises the rationalist practice of reductionism otherwise known as scientific management. All the functions described in the table above relate to the formulation and execution of a plan in a predictable climate and indicate why radical and unexpected changes to the anticipated operating environment disrupt the model. Usually these plans are based on data for earlier periods but are implemented in a subsequent period in which the operating environment will have changed, but only in subtle ways, that differ from that predicted.

When the economic system encounters a recession or some other significant negative event such as a major war (known as a high impact, low probability event or HILPE) then changes to the operating environment become rapid, occasionally sudden, and the effect on organisations can be so profound that the basic condition of stability that underpins management's rational processes is absent.

Kotter's functions contain no comment about building in flexibility and adaptability that allow the plan to evolve. He tends to be concerned only with the rectification of deviations from the plan to enable the agreed programme to get back on track. Something that is probably not feasible when turbulence is encountered.

Having observed the catastrophic virtual collapse of the world financial system in 2008 and the precipitous descent into global recession we are forced to conclude that either:

1. Drucker and Kotter were wrong and that the economic environment is not a knowable and controllable place.

2. Those charged with the management of the system have abandoned the techniques designed to maintain control.

3. The techniques themselves are deficient.

I suggest that most of the answer lies in 1 and 3 above.

The world economic system is not like a machine in which the function, behaviour and relationship to one another of the component parts can be described in mechanistic terms. In recent years we have come to understand that it is a complex system that behaves in a chaotic way,[7] like the weather or a crowd of people leaving a stadium, and that it is prone to sudden and apparently unpredictable changes.

It is difficult to control a dynamic system that you cannot predict and for this reason alone management, during times of turmoil, cannot rely on the systematic tools that they use when the world seems a more reliable place.

The established techniques of management science seem to work in the spring and summer of the business cycle but become unreliable in the winter.

In turbulent times the urgent time frame of action and the necessity to modify plans and budgets in response to unexpected events added to the possibility of their 'out of trend' scale cannot be accommodated by the rigid adherence to established processes on which scientific management depends.

Yet the ultimate test of management is performance. Achievement rather than comprehension remains, of necessity, the aim. Management, in other words, is a practice, rather than a science or a profession, although it contains elements of both.

Indeed, I suggest that if managing in stable periods is a science then in turbulent times it is more of an art.

---

[7] Technically it is defined as a non-linear dynamic system.

The managerial toolkit

My concern about the dependability of the 'tools' of management science is such an important point that I need to offer a little more justification.

I do not want you to feel that I am stripping you of all weapons and armour at the moment when you are about to go into battle. But neither do I want you to believe that wooden shields are going to stop bullets.

When the turbulence is particular to your company, in other words the external environment is not turbulent but for whatever reason your company encounters a destabilising event, then the tools of management science continue to be dependable.

This type of problem can be defined clearly and often can be dealt with as if it were a broken part in a machine, with reasonable confidence that the external environment is not going to change significantly over the timescale in which remedial action is planned.

Of course the problem you encounter may be of such severity that it cannot be resolved or the shape of the company cannot be preserved in its current form.

For example, the failure to derive the anticipated benefits from a major acquisition leaves the combined business with all the costs but without the rewards to pay them. Plan A has failed and must be abandoned. Plan B must adopt less ambitious benefits with the objective of making the new financial structure bearable. The conventional managerial toolkit is at its most effective in such circumstances provided significant deterioration in the operating conditions is not the primary cause of the trouble.

I want you to appreciate that in turbulent times the challenges you will confront are unpredictable and while your established techniques will be useful weapons against swords and spears, they will have little effect on an unspecific enemy who deploys its technologically superior weapons from a distance beyond your reach. To survive and emerge unscathed you will need other tools.

The set of tools on which managers rely are based on rational quasi-scientific methods of analysis and deduction. They were developed to be applicable to a wide range of enterprises and organisations and are based on the presumption that the problems managers encounter are not necessarily industry specific but are universal, and the range is finite. The managerial confidence that equips people to control complex, multi-location, diverse companies is built on the presumption that most problems they may encounter will be susceptible to treatment with this standard 'toolkit' of procedures.

For this to be a viable proposition dissimilarities must be either insignificant or irrelevant and the 'workbench' on which these universal tools are used must be stable.

Let me illustrate this point with an analogy. A surgeon uses a scalpel as part of her standard toolkit. This is a low-tech reliable implement that she uses with confidence. However, her confidence is based on the expectation that the patient will be immobilised and the operating table will be stable. The surgeon cannot have the same confidence if the patient or the operating table are moving unpredictably.

Similarly, the tools used with confidence by management in stable times cannot be used with equivalent confidence in turbulent times.

When local turbulence is either caused by or arises simultaneously with external instability then the tools of management science become less reliable. But in either case it is pointless agonising over your preference or what might have been. The situation has changed and the status quo ante cannot be recreated.

When a company encounters difficulties at a time of general economic turbulence the problems management faces are similar to the surgeon and the scalpel. All the elements in the picture are the same but the turbulence renders the previously dependable tool unreliable. If you are unable to stabilise the turmoil you cannot use the tool with confidence.

Managers are trained and encouraged to approach each problem in a manner which enables them to apply one of the methodologies contained within their toolkit. This is understandable because the tools, such as budgeting, strategic planning, management by objectives, discounted cash flow analysis, SWOT analysis, etc. all appear powerful and universally applicable. Moreover, the problem cannot be ignored and if there are no better tools available you must utilise those you have.

If you are a surgeon you may turn to the scalpel because you have no knowledge or experience of non-invasive procedures. But there is danger in shaping the problem to fit the tools available.

The managerial toolkit will also be deficient if it is applied to a problem that falls outside the scope of regularly occurring problems for which it was designed. A scalpel is unlikely to cure influenza. An irregular or novel problem will, therefore, in all probability be approached inadequately by a manager if he or she possesses neither the specialist tools nor the experience that are appropriate.

This incompatibility between the set of managerial competencies and the situation to which they are applied arises most conspicuously at times of significant change. The turbulence and comparative unpredictability of such times renders inadequate the technical processes of management designed to impose control during less turbulent times when change is moderate and incremental.

Returning to our surgeon and scalpel analogy, what can be done? Must the patient die because the turbulence prevents the surgeon using her scalpel with confidence? Or should the surgeon use the scalpel even though she knows it is the wrong tool?

You may not be able to calm the turbulence but you can reduce its effect by installing an inertial dampening system. However, if you cannot stabilise the patient, the table and yourself sufficiently then you must abandon the scalpel and find a new tool. You can attempt another procedure that is less invasive or a non-surgical regime to stabilise the patient until the turbulence reduces sufficiently for the scalpel to be used. Of course some procedures are too urgent to wait and there is no satisfactory alternative. In these cases the surgeon has no choice but to do the best she can because the patient will certainly die without immediate action and they may survive even if it's an imperfect procedure.

Of course you must also be pragmatic. You may conclude that the effects of turbulence can be eradicated sufficiently to perform surgery almost normally if you can construct a gyroscopically controlled operating room, but that is not a practical proposition.

So, you must accept that the best available action may be sub-optimal, but if you do nothing the patient will die and hence your less than perfect option increases the chance of the patient's survival especially if you can envisage some of the possible setbacks that you may encounter during the procedure and prepare compensatory action.

In other words you must be creative and evaluate more options than would normally be the case if you were confronted by the same problem in less turbulent times.

Change versus control

Management is about imposing and maintaining control through the practice of compartmentalisation and compliance with a set of laws and rules. But this requires a comparatively slow pace of change that facilitates the rational and systematic evaluation of recent trends and where their continuation might lead. So the kind of rapid, unpredictable change that characterises turbulent times is anathema.

Managers embrace progress as an objective but only where it can be accomplished through incremental change. They tend to be comparatively risk averse, departmentally myopic and protective, and place a premium on reactionary rational adaptation.

The consequence of this mindset and conduct is that, through their advocacy or rejection of projects, managers tend to guide organisations away from situations where fundamental change is necessary. Radical change is turbulent and risky and is the antithesis of their preferred methodology and comfort position.

Most managers can, to some extent, predict and deal with the regular and moderate variations in the general operating climate, but few are trained adequately to deal with conditions analogous to earthquakes and hurricanes.

Their forecasts of the near future are usually based on an extrapolation of recent trends. Statistically this is a valid procedure as, for most of the time, the probability is high that the next period will be a function of preceding periods. It is also difficult to detect the green shoots of growing turbulence amongst the verdant undergrowth of a fertile market economy.

An uncertain future and concerns about the lack of control can cause managers to be biased towards the avoidance or denial of the need for fundamental or radical change. In fact the nature of managerial training, perspective and the toolkit combine to render some managers blind to the emerging signals of significant or discontinuous change.

It is sometimes also suggested that the actions of managers lead inevitably to organisational decline and are the cause of the kind of transitional events they prefer to avoid. Their desire for control imposes inflexibility on an organisation and inhibits its capacity to deform and adapt naturally or easily in response to turbulent changes in its operating environment.

Only when the need for change is imposed by the emergence of external events such as those encountered during 2008 do managers have no option but to confront turbulence and change.

Leaving aside the question of whether or not conventional managerial conduct can be a principal cause of the need for reform, it is apparent that organisational difficulties can be exacerbated by a manager's over-reliance on the techniques that served him or her well in stable times. The response to the unusual problems that arise from an organisation's turbulent incompatibility with its operating environment must not be limited to or even be led by the more strenuous application of these conventional processes.

The conventional processes are the scientific management tools which managers have become accustomed to using to ply their trade. These were designed to function in an age when our economic system was less interconnected and somewhat slower paced. It is not surprising, therefore, that they do not seem to work as well today as they have in the past.

The conventional practice reaches its effective limit in turbulent times when the pace of change is more rapid than the conventional toolkit can control.

It is, in part, this analysis which leads to the conclusion that managers should confine the time of their greatest influence to periods of relative stability. These are punctuated by turbulent periods of significant change (transitional events) and it is during these turbulent periods when managers are seemingly less effective and people begin to distinguish between managers and leaders and look for the latter.

Doing the right thing or doing things right?

Managers tend to regard 'doing things right' as implementing those procedures and techniques that they have been taught or learned through experience.

But established methodologies are not necessarily equally effective in all situations. Management is not like physics in which certain immutable and universally applicable laws establish a reliable set of founding principles.

So it does not follow that the emergence of turmoil results from managers being lax in their diligent application of techniques. Nor does it follow that turbulence can be ameliorated or its consequences avoided by adopting a more conscientious application of the established techniques of management science. The 'right thing' to do is not the same as 'doing things right'.

Doing the right thing means being aware of the abnormality of the situation, the degree to which conventional tools are effective and the extent to which your experience is appropriate.

In turbulent times you cannot restore stability by the avoidance of action, nor do you want to be pressurised into acting from panic.

Avoiding panic moves

Individuals are programmed to believe that inaction in the face of clear and present danger is not the most appropriate conduct.

If a car is driving towards you then to hold your ground seems to be a stupid decision likely to result in you being injured. But jumping off a high bridge in panic to avoid the car is equally irrational.

The virtuous act of facing down the threat has absolutely no effect, nor does pretending that it is irrelevant. Turbulent times are insensitive to the reputation, stature or posturing of the manager.

Managers should not deny or ignore the emergence of turbulent times or minimise the risks to their organisation but nor should they believe that, having concluded that a dangerous storm is developing, they must be seen to be doing something even though it is a poorly considered action.

Doing something because you must oppose the onslaught and this is the only action you can envisage that may have any effect is insufficient.

Ill-considered action may result in irreparable damage in the same way that sailing a boat badly in a storm can be disastrous. Running with the sea is, in some conditions, just as destabilising as running against it. If going sideways is just as bad or not an option what action do you as the manager/helmsman take?

Most experienced sailors will say that if you are in turbulent water that is unfamiliar to you, then you must learn to read the sea and try to position the boat differently in anticipation of the next wave. All waves are not the same and each must be dealt with on its merits. Adaptability is the necessary attribute. Take a series of small decisions until you can make a strategic move with confidence.

Avoiding inaction

Inaction sometimes seems to be the best option simply because all the other possibilities are replete with risks that you as a manager do not seem able to control.

To continue the boating analogy; the storm is upon you, your GPS system doesn't work, you have no charts, you're unfamiliar with the conditions and do not know in which direction safety lies. You have no means of determining which of the options available is best as they all seem potentially risky. A voyage into the unknown. So rather than panic and choose a direction at random you adopt the natural rational human tendency to do nothing unless it appears to offer a clear potential for improving the status quo lest the action you take makes matters worse.

But inaction in the hope of a clearer picture emerging in which you are able to make a rational decision is also highly risky. You may be swamped by the next big wave, the storm may get worse, you may be driven onto rocks, you may be washed overboard, etc.

An understanding of your managerial psychology is a key component in determining the right course of action. You must identify in yourself whether you are being driven to ill-considered activity or inactivity by panic or fear, and factor your emotional state and that of your colleagues into your decision-making process.

If you are inexperienced and the conditions are unfamiliar and hostile, maintaining the maximum flexibility is paramount in case your initial action proves to be wrong.

In turbulent times taking some action is better than taking no action, but failing to recognise the wrong action and not being brave enough or sufficiently flexible to abandon this and adopt a different course is a cardinal error.

Rather than allowing yourself to be consumed by the detail of the current manifestations of the problems you are facing, I suggest that understanding the position of your organisation and the prevailing managerial psychology are the necessary starting points.

You must have an objective assessment of where your organisation lies on its lifespan to determine the characteristics that may inhibit your capacity to implant change. For example, in the UK Woolworths spent perhaps 25 of its 99 years in decline following a long period of maturity. Despite frequent changes of senior management it became seemingly impossible for it to adapt and to abandon its entrenched but no longer viable proposition. Incremental change was perused as if the business was in maturity when what was needed, but resisted forcefully, was radical change in recognition of decline.

Early into the recession of 2008/09 Woolworths collapsed.

You must address turbulence differently depending on the phase of its lifespan your organisation is in.

3

Corporate lifespan

Change is the constant condition of the physical universe. Some things change so slowly that they appear constant but then unexpectedly vary significantly and suddenly. But if there was no capacity for major or unpredictable change there would be no novelty and no progress.

Our economic system is similar and within it the role of management is not to eliminate change but to moderate the pace to a level at which progress, that is incremental constructive change, can be induced as the persistent state.

But the notion of progress implies the replacement of one thing with something new and preferable. Hence the product, process, service or distribution channel that is superseded must either adapt or die.

This constant churning, the dance of progress, follows a pattern that applies to all things.

Sometimes this change is turbulent, occasionally it is the result of unexpected and unpredictable events but it also arises naturally in the transit between the sequence of phases an organisation encounters as it evolves along its lifespan.

The life*span*, sometimes misleadingly called the life cycle, describes the way an organisation grows, matures and declines. The way it lives its life and dies and, in particular, the crises, both natural and unexpected, that it encounters which shape and colour the organisation as it ages just as similar events mould our own lives.

Few organisations, if any, enjoy an incident free or turbulent free lifespan. If they reach the phase of maturity they will encounter at least one economic recession and with it externally induced turbulence. If they do not reach maturity then they will encounter the turbulence of premature decline and collapse.

The corporate lifespan illustrated below provides the basic model along which leadership and management must function as the company encounters, in turn, the need for change or consolidation.

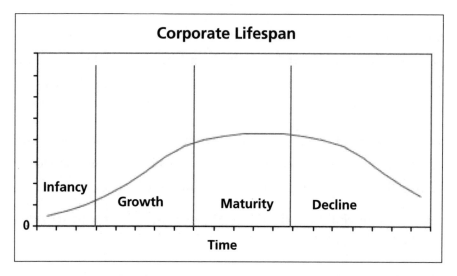

© Anthony Holmes 2004

The natural turbulent turning points are the transitional events that arise when a company moves from its growth phase into maturity and the change from maturity to decline. The change to maturity marks the need for managerial skills to replace the pioneering attributes that have been employed to found and grow the company, and marks the point at which the managerial challenge changes to control what has, through success, become growth in excess of system capacity which, unless it is controlled, will lead to failure.

The movement from maturity into decline may result from the ossifying control imposed by management which has inhibited the organisation's capacity to adapt rapidly to environmental changes (as per the Woolworths example given earlier). This drift is usually signalled by declining profit, reduced cash flow and increased income gearing.

The psychological mode of management that characterises each phase in the lifespan can be described simply as follows:

Lifespan Phase	Mode
Infancy	Beginning
Growth	Becoming
Maturity	Being
Decline	Reversing

Beginning	The organisation is born and the management orientation is focussed on ensuring that it becomes sufficiently established in its landscape to allow it to sustain a viable existence.
Becoming	Management is concerned primarily with achieving what the organisation is, according to their assessment, capable of becoming.
Being	Having grown to the stage at which additional marginal expansion declines and further substantial organic growth is unlikely, management turns to maximising the value to be extracted from being.
Reversing	In a climate of decline when the prognosis may be organisational demise, incumbent management is initially concerned with returning to the preceding state of stable maturity. You might regard it as controversial to suggest that the more appropriate psychology mode is 'becoming' and that the failure to recognise this explains why incumbent management sometimes are less able to operate successfully in this phase than are new individuals who look only forward.

Managers generally predict a steady state over the short to medium term and, as a result, fail to anticipate the emergence of a turning point that leads to a transitional event and to begin an orderly modification in the managerial mode in recognition of the need for significant change and the turbulence that may accompany it.

In addition to these natural turbulent phase transitions, high impact low probability events (HILPEs) also create, often unexpected, crises that are also transitional events and create the need to change the managerial style.

Using the conventional description of the corporate lifespan as a base enables managers and stakeholders to understand the points at which turbulence will arise naturally, and the phases during which reliance on the procedures established to control the recent phase lose their saliency.

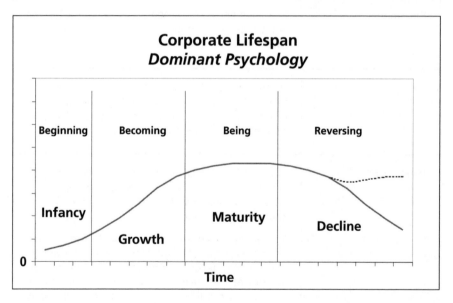

© Anthony Holmes 2004

Of course, this is a very simplified illustration. The lifespan of each firm is different and for those that reach maturity the duration of this phase often exceeds the period of growth.

However, all firms experience periods of comparatively rapid change that are usually positive in the early phases and negative in later stages. Resistance to these changes is, as they say, futile, nonetheless it is natural although perhaps less pronounced in the transition from growth to maturity than from maturity into decline.

The early period is a stage of building and capitalising on what has been achieved. The later period is negative and necessitates the painful discontinuation of things once considered important, perhaps the contraction of the organisation, a reduction in staff, etc., etc.

In fact many of the things that were established as desirable when 'becoming' and 'being' dominated the psychology now become impediments to survival.

Lifespans differ in length and shape and a few companies manage to reinvent themselves by recognising their imminent demise due to the dwindling availability of what they need to survive. In those that do so their managers adopt a psychology of a second phase of 'becoming'. They pursue a new viable position rather than attempting to return to the status quo ante, which is usually not possible.

The dotted line in the figure opposite in the decline phase represents the desired change in trend which I contend can only be sought if management changes the natural psychology of 'reversing' to 'becoming'.

Take, for example, the postal services. In 1635 Charles I gave the general public access to the royal mail system. This was a novel and expensive system of communication limited by the speed a horse could travel. In its lifespan a number of challenges have confronted its management. The advent of railways, enabling the unit cost of posting a letter to reduce and the speed of delivery to increase, stimulated an expansion in demand and the volume of letters, which was further magnified by an increase in literacy. Telegraphy, wireless telegraphy and then telephony caused the market to change, at first slowly and then turbulently.

Now, the advent of modern telecoms and broadband connectivity has begun to undermine hard copy communication. ISP's have no legacy assets or culture to manage out of and their managerial psychology is 'becoming', whereas the objective of postal companies is to moderate the rate at which hard copy communication decays so that they can manage their decline in an orderly manner.

They have transcended the mature phase of 'being' and are now firmly entrenched in decline. Reversal is clearly not a viable strategy, which leaves orderly demise or 'becoming'. No one doubts that 'becoming' is difficult and perhaps more so for managers who have spent many years in maturity immersed in the procedures of 'being', but there are notable examples of companies that have left behind their previous shape and nature to 'become' something new and viable. IBM is a good example that has accomplished this transition from mechanical computational machines to electronic computers to software development.

As an industrial society we have faced, and continue to deal with the legacy of, the decline in large-scale employment industries such as mineral extraction and processing, volume manufacturing of standardised products, and utilities such as the postal services. Many economists argue that the principal impediment to the transition to new industries is labour inflexibility, which resists the decline in their staple industry until it collapses catastrophically with unpleasant social consequences for many who continue to be wholly dependent on these businesses.

Although simplified, the proposition is clear; try to resist the natural change from one lifespan phase to another and the probability is that you will amplify the turbulence inherent in the transition and most likely fail as the forces that drive the lifespan process are beyond management's control. Resistance is futile.

Only external factors can distort the sequence by either bringing forward the turning points (e.g. the firm loses business when a technically superior replacement enters the market) or, potentially retarding them (e.g. the firm wins business unexpectedly when the industry structure changes as a competitor fails).

* * * *

Transitional events, because they are turbulent, are often regarded as 'negative' periods as the continual incremental progress, which is the 'positive' objective of scientific management, is suspended and reform becomes necessary.

When the rate of growth diminishes marking the transition from growth to maturity or profit declines indicating the transition to decline, managers tend to regard the changes negatively as they assess the present and future in comparison with a more successful past. They often conceive of objectives in terms of returning to this state, which is why you hear calls to 'get back to basics' as though the fault that needs to be rectified is some deviation from previous practice, and when this toxic component has been excised, the company will perform as it did in the past.

But in a recession the future is another country and severe economic turbulence often signals a discontinuity rather than a pause and creates a turning point of such significance that what emerges cannot easily be connected to the trends of the preceding years.

Reversing is not possible. This is a one-way street and managers who drive the corporate vehicle forward while looking through the rear view mirror will not progress far without hitting an obstacle. The faster they accelerate to escape the undesirable conditions the more damaging the inevitable crash will be.

Identifying an organisation's position in its lifespan

Identifying an organisation's position in its lifespan is not easily achieved in a precise way. Ideally, those charged with the direction of the organisation would like to predict the impending onset of each point at which the rate of progression changes, heralding the movement from growth to maturity and from maturity to decline. Where this is possible plans can be made to address the specific issues that are associated with these transitional phases.

Some businesses never reach maturity and disappear from the corporate landscape a few months or years after their introduction. For these organisations spending time looking for the signs of transition is irrelevant as they are destined never to reach critical mass. Many of these will be too immature to survive turbulent times. The fortunate few may be sold to larger companies who are better able to withstand the turmoil. Others will just fall by the wayside.

Calculating the scale that a business needs to achieve in order for it to become established and escape its beginning and confront its becoming is a relatively simple calculation. The point at which it consistently generates cash rather than consumes it is an important signal. The period in which revenue growth accelerates and profits are made and begin to grow at a faster rate than revenue grows is another notable pattern.

When these rates of growth begin to diminish it suggests another transitional stage is approaching.

If one of these natural turning points occurs during a time of general turbulence then the organisational turmoil can be immense and be beyond the manager's capacity to cope in an orderly way. In general, however, it is usually difficult to identify these points with certainty until they are past and action is directed at the management of the consequences rather than their avoidance or mitigation.

I do not believe that this is sufficient reason simply to ignore these phases and adopt the position that it is impossible to put in place a strategy to address each stage leaving, instead, reactionary tactics as the only viable methodology.

Let me suggest how the approximate position of the organisation in its lifespan can be determined by initially eliminating the phases in which the organisation is *not* located.

Transit along the lifespan is mostly unidirectional. The early stage of growth is followed by maturity, which precedes decline. By definition decline does not proceed the early stage of growth, although some organisations fail to enjoy a prolonged period of maturity and appear to enter decline shortly after growth ends. Examples of these are organisations and products launched to capitalise on highly fashionable trends or transitory technology such as fan clubs for popular music bands, children's toys, some financial products based on tax breaks, some software products, vacation resorts, trendy restaurants, TV shows and movies. For these types of organisation the whole of their lives are turbulent as they never encounter the relative stability of a prolonged period of maturity.

The duration of each phase will vary and be different for each organisation but empirical evidence suggests that in a large number of cases (such as fashion products) the more rapid the growth phase the shorter the period of maturity and more rapid the onset of decline.

The presumption that, if unmanaged, the lifespan curve is symmetrical – taking the shape of a normal distribution – is a reasonable starting point. However, empirical evidence reveals that decline to collapse occurs at an accelerating rate and is steeper than the change from infancy to growth. Economic recessions and HILPEs tend to magnify this end stage asymmetry.

A feedback system works at this point. The onset of decline causes organisational turbulence and the emergence of environmental turbulence, such as a recession, tends to accelerate the decline of businesses in late maturity by magnifying their problems, causing additional turbulence in its wake and reducing the options for rectification.

A determination of whether it is likely that the organisation is in maturity or decline may be made by considering what the preceding phase is most likely to have been.

If the organisation is in maturity or decline it will exhibit characteristics that cannot be mistaken for those of an immature organisation in the infancy or growth phase. Some of these characteristics of infancy and growth are obvious:

- The company is still comparatively new and has probably commenced trading within the preceding five years.

- Revenue growth in the last two years will be significantly greater than any preceding period.

- Headcount will have grown to add human capacity to manage the enlarged business.

- Capital spending will probably have been high in relation to the company's scale and the company will have moved premises at least once in the preceding three years to add physical capacity.

- A significant fraction of revenue growth will be attributable to the acquisition of new customers and not through increased demand from existing buyers.

- Most of the senior management team will have been with the company since its early days.

- Because the business is expanding quickly the process is probably disorganised and turbulent.

If the company doesn't have these characteristics the early stage may be discounted and it may be concluded that the organisation is located in the maturity or decline phase. The following are some of the characteristics that indicate a move to maturity and beyond:

- The company will have existed for longer than five years. It is unlikely that a company that has survived for a longer period, probably in a buoyant economy, remains in its infancy.

- Historical revenue growth will reveal a phase of expansion at a rate higher than in preceding years followed, most recently, by a phase of more modest or no growth.

- Return on capital will for several years have 'normalised' to close to the industry average and now additional capital will be required.

- Recent profit growth will have been solid rather than spectacular and a loss may be predicted.

If the preceding phase was growth and no discernable period of consolidation or stagnation has been experienced then it is possible but unlikely that the organisation moved from the early stage straight to decline. It is more likely that the organisation has entered maturity.

Early maturity is preceded by recent slowing growth. Late maturity is characterised by recent low growth, stagnation or oscillation between slow growth and intermittent periods of decline.

It is unnecessary to conduct further analysis if there are prima facie indications of late maturity or decline and the general economic environment is turbulent or predicted to be so. In such circumstances management should assume difficulties lie ahead and begin to act accordingly.

This elimination of phase methodology becomes unreliable when only very recent data are used so at least five data points are needed covering a minimum period of 2½ years. These data may be distorted by recent fluctuations within a phase thereby giving the misleading impression that the organisation is in maturity when it is just encountering a pause in growth and the pattern of expansion will resume.

Sometimes complex systems, like the economy or a market, seem to settle briefly at an equilibrium point but then, for no easily apparent reason, they resume momentum, occasionally not in line with the previous trend.

It is also feasible to determine your company's lifespan position in general terms by evaluating the mode of management, i.e. whether it is concerned predominantly with 'becoming' or with 'being'. However, the problem with this subjective appraisal is that, at the turning point from one phase to the next, it is often difficult to form a conclusive judgement.

How to determine the managerial mode

This is a subject that could consume the pages of another book and therefore I do not intend to attempt a comprehensive discussion in this brief work. By the same token I do not want to be so superficial that you conclude that there are just a few easily recognised traits that will enable a clear identification of the prevalent mode.

The key mode to search for is denial, which I discuss in a little more depth in chapter 4.

The point I want to emphasise is that the action you take in turbulent times depends not just on your organisation's position in its lifespan or the psychological mode of management but on the way the two interact.

If the organisation's position in its lifespan is late maturity or early decline, it is a period of general economic uncertainty and an appraisal of management's psychology concludes that denial or concealment of problems is the dominant condition, then stakeholders should consider the early removal of the incumbent senior management and the replacing of them with individuals experienced in leading unstable businesses.

If the same external conditions are encountered during the growth phase and managers are engaged in the self-deception of denial as to do otherwise means an admission that their ambitions may be unfulfilled then, as the senior manager, you must examine the consequences of growth being truncated. Will the scale achieved be sufficient to give the critical mass necessary for maturity or can the investment in growth be slowed until more conducive conditions return? Will 'becoming' be brought to a premature end and are you organised enough to enter the mode of 'being'?

These preliminary comments lead directly into the important area of managerial psychology and the mindset managers need to understand and adopt in order to manage through turbulent times.

4

Psychology of management

The psychology of those individuals in command changes significantly as their organisation proceeds along its lifespan from origination, through a phase of growth into one of consolidation and perhaps complacency (maturity), to be followed by decline.

The turbulence that arises as an organisation moves from one phase of its lifespan to the next, and particularly in the moves from infancy to growth and decline to the crisis that precedes collapse, modifies the manager's state of mind, although the change often occurs too slowly for the individual to be aware that an alteration has taken place. Only when an external event induces extraordinarily rapid change (a HILPE) is the altered psychological state noticeable over a short period.

There is an obvious analogy in the change in psychology that occurs during the human lifespan. As an individual moves through adolescence to maturity their psychology changes gradually from turbulent self-consciousness and assertiveness to the mature assuredness, and for some resignation, that comes with finding a place in the world.

But when a significant and unexpected event, such as the death of someone close or serious illness, disturbs this natural progression the change in the person's psychology is profound, rapid and sometimes permanent.

In passing you may wish to contemplate whether corporate management should follow the example of the medical profession and recognise that dealing with the problems of youth is a specialist activity that requires an expertise different to that applied to those in late middle and old age, which also has its own specialist practitioners. There is no established genre of 'paediatric' management or 'geriatric' management. Although I have heard the latter term used as a pejorative adjective!

An important observation is that organisational turbulence tends to be driven by the simultaneous emergence of several problems in response to which managers conceive contradictory actions that they are unable to reconcile or order objectively. Consequently unity dissipates, political conflict emerges and team cohesion is lost as managers form factions, each of which has an ideological preference for one or other incompatible proposal.

Each group fears that taking the wrong action will create an irretrievably dire situation and hence, if the organisational power is well balanced between them, each vetoes or blocks actions advocated by other groups and the organisation stagnates. The most expedient way in which to break this deadlock is to import an external senior executive who holds no allegiance to any faction but has the authority to determine the action that must be taken.

Managing through turbulent times is likely to be the most challenging activity a manager will confront. Corporate turmoil and distress is testing if it arises during a period when the economic climate is stable or positive. The managerial demands are magnified when difficulties arise in a time of recession, when economic activity declines and the availability of finance is restricted and, often, inflation is rampant. These combine to extend and complicate the equation that managers have to solve.

As external conditions deteriorate most managers begin, reluctantly, to think about how the growing turbulence will affect their business. Many of the variables in the big complex equation begin to change unpredictably. This is a managerial nightmare. It induces anxiety and stress and it is not surprising that the psychology of managers changes, although their conduct might appear to remain relatively constant.

Indeed, you might conclude that any manager who continues to behave as if unconcerned about a generally predicted deterioration in the operating environment is exhibiting an inappropriate psychological mode. As is the manager who is panicked into premature or ill-considered action by the possibility of turbulent times.

Adverse economic conditions tend to expose the vulnerabilities of organisations that are in early growth or early decline and push them into crises more rapidly than companies in maturity.

Mature companies with established markets, systems and procedures often fall into decline because the impact of some unanticipated negative event cannot be addressed adequately or rapidly as it falls outside of the established systems' capability or management's preparation for specific future conditions.

Managers of companies in maturity also tend to have been in position for a longer period than their counterparts in immature businesses or those in decline. As a result they often become unable to deal effectively with conditions in which many variables change rapidly and in unpredictable ways.

The following table illustrates in rather more detail how the managerial mode is conditioned by the phase of the lifespan the organisation is passing through.

Phase of Lifespan	Mode	Psychology
Infancy	Beginning	Confidence, anticipation, expansive
Growth	Becoming #1	
Maturity	Being	Complacency, preservation, reactionary
Decline	Reversing/Becoming #2	Fear, reversion, escape
Crisis/collapse	Avoiding	

In the early stages of an organisation's life those directing the enterprise tend to be unified and motivated by their anticipation of the rewards that they believe lie ahead and plan for. There is no historical record from which they have deduced patterns and taken learnings about actions that work and those that have failed. Hence they approach most issues with an open mind and, in consequence, are more likely to be adaptive and to formulate novel solutions.

The individuals directing the organisation during this phase have much to gain and little to lose so they tend to move forward and take risks with confidence.

At some point the comparative freedom that attends the early stage begins to be replaced by the need to bureaucratise and consolidate what has been achieved. The memory of past successes and failures influences decision-making with greater weight and new challenges are progressively evaluated through the prism of this experience.

Most managers begin to adopt a mode of increasing risk adversity in which they are repelled by taking the large gamble of introducing novel products and expansionary developments such as new factories, overseas expansion and acquisitions which 'bet the company'.

When critical mass has been achieved and growth slows, the organisation enters a phase of maturity during which the default objective is to preserve the organisation and to maintain profitability (*being* replaces *becoming*) and the phase of rapid growth ends. The processes and systems installed to control the volume of activity that has been built during the pioneering phase begin to function efficiently. Those individuals who are minded to take large risks and are able to manage turbulence and may agitate to move the business to a new destination (sometimes called a charismatic leader) tend to be avoided in favour of the type of manager who exudes an emphasis on control and gradualism.

In maturity the lifespan line is, more or less, horizontal and therefore in this relatively stable state the techniques of management science are at their most effective and policy can be set in the reasonable expectation that the characteristics of next year will be similar to those of this year.

The repetitive nature of the actions taken within this phase leads to complacency as the predominant psychological state.

The psychology becomes increasingly risk-averse as managers are disinclined to gamble what has been achieved in pursuit of more than incremental growth.

But history reveals that product range extensions and other low-risk moves have only a limited potential for driving growth. They follow the law of diminishing marginal returns to scale in which the nth move yields less than the $n\text{-}1^{th}$.

So managerial psychology contributes strongly to the creation of the frozen business model that characterises maturity.

Fixed systems and processes militate against change, instil caution, moderate and eventually minimise the organisation's adaptive capability. The consequence is that, as the operating environment evolves other, newer organisations emerge to challenge the mature and complacent incumbents. These newcomers are at the early stage of their lifespan and are directed by individuals whose frame of mind is anticipatory and comparatively less risk-averse.

It is the battle between the 'being' of maturity in the established business and the 'becoming' of infancy in the newcomer. A battle which the former's now self-satisfied and complacent managers once experienced from the position of 'becoming' and in which they prospered to reach maturity. Those who experienced both phases in the same organisation may come to believe that the struggle of 'becoming' has earned them a place in the less challenging managerial sun of maturity and they are not interested in, and will actively avoid recognising, a resurgence of turbulent times.

The newcomers to the market apply pressure on the incumbent players who are unable to counteract with the necessary immediacy as they are less adaptive and unwilling to abandon the sunk cost in financial and emotional capital invested in their established methodology.

The mature business starts to lose ground and its guiding minds find their psychology begins to be dominated by fear of the conditions that will obtain if the observed trend of decline continues.

At this point the senior management exhibits a characteristic pattern of behavioural traits. Initially, their complacency causes challenges to be met with an arrogant dismissal that the newcomers will provide an insufficient challenge to their enterprise to cause any destabilisation.

Here is an amusing story, fictional I think, that a friend emailed to illustrate the kind of deluded thinking that can arise.

A Japanese company (T) and an American company (F) decided to have a canoe race on the Missouri River. Both teams practiced long and hard to reach their peak performance before the race.

On the big day, the Japanese won by a mile.

The Americans, very discouraged and depressed, decided to investigate the reason for the crushing defeat. A management team made up of senior management was formed to investigate and recommend appropriate action.

Their conclusion was the Japanese had 8 people rowing and 1 person steering, while the American team had 7 people steering and 2 people rowing.

Feeling a deeper study was in order, American management hired a consulting company and paid them a large amount of money for a second opinion.

They advised, of course, that too many people were steering the boat, while not enough people were rowing.

Not sure of how to utilize that information but wanting to prevent another loss to the Japanese, the rowing team's management structure was totally reorganized to 4 steering supervisors, 2 area steering superintendents and 1 assistant superintendent steering manager.

They also implemented a new performance system that would give the 2 people rowing the boat greater incentive to work harder. It was called the 'Rowing Team Quality First Program,' with meetings, dinners and free pens for the rowers. There was discussion of getting new paddles, canoes and other equipment, extra vacation days for practices and bonuses. The pension program was trimmed to 'equal the competition' and some of the resultant savings were channelled into morale boosting programs and teamwork posters.

The next year the Japanese won by two miles.

Humiliated, the American management laid-off one rower, halted development of a new canoe, sold all the paddles, and cancelled all capital investments for new equipment. The money saved was distributed to the senior executives as bonuses.

The next year, try as he might, the lone designated rower was unable to even finish the race (having no paddles) so he was laid off for unacceptable performance. All canoe equipment was sold and the next year's racing team was outsourced to India.

Sadly, the End.

Here's something else to think about: F has spent the last thirty years moving all its factories out of the US, claiming they can't make money paying American wages.

T has spent the last thirty years building more than a dozen plants inside the US. The last quarter's results:

- T makes $4 billion in profits while F racked up $9 billion in losses.

- F is driven by the psychology of 'being' and T by 'becoming'.

The psychology of managers varies from confidence to doubt in proportion to the degree of certainty they perceive in their understanding of the linkages between cause and effect. Their preferred state is to achieve consensus and harmony within the management team. Indeed, in the 1970s and 1980s when Japan was considered to be the benchmark for modern management it was noted that a Japanese company would tend not to proceed with a project until a consensus and therefore harmony had been achieved.

For every manager the ideal situation arises when:

1. Belief is high that key causal relationships are understood and hence the managerial toolkit can be applied with confidence.

2. There is also a high level of harmony amongst the management team.

Ralph Stacey[8] has taken the relationship between these conditions to illustrate the way in which managerial behaviour should change. I have modified the resulting matrix in order to create the following Turbulence Matrix (T-matrix):

---

[8] Ralph Stacey; Professor of Management and Director of the Complexity and Management Centre at the Business School of the University of Hertfordshire.

The T-Matrix

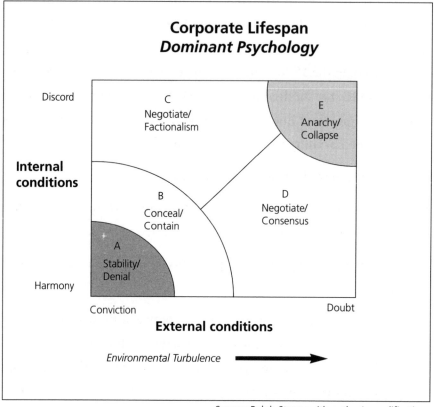

Source: Ralph Stacey with author's modifications

A = Management is unified and confident of its understanding of external dynamics. This is often the position of mature organisations in a stable economic environment and is the position in which the danger of complacency resides.

B = Management is less confident and unified and experiences anxiety and anticipation. This is the position of organisations in infancy and growth.

C & D = Complexity. The dangerous corridor of uncertainty in which complexity grows and certainty diminishes noticeably. Organisations in crisis or decline are positioned in these zones.

C = The position when turbulence is the result of managerial disunity and factional infighting disables the organisation's response to deteriorating external conditions. Extremely stressful.

D = Deteriorating external conditions begin to overwhelm management although the team remains unified. High levels of anxiety.

E = Chaos. The organisation is beginning to disintegrate as it confronts extreme complexity in a disorganised and uncoordinated way. Organisations positioned in this zone are in serious decline and are close to collapse. Fear and panic dominate.

In the Appendix I discuss briefly how to determine an organisation's position on each axis.

It is vitally important for the senior management of an organisation that is entering turbulent times to recognise changes in their psychology. Doing so is not easy as the modifications tend to emerge as small changes that are readily dismissed as someone 'having a bad day'. Excuses are made and the new conduct is frequently absorbed to become the general nature of things. The difficulty of identifying crucial psychological changes underlines the importance of consulting someone with an objective perspective who is able to compare metrics of a manager's beliefs and attitudes from preceding periods.

The ease with which factionalism can develop from healthy debate in the presence of contradictory choices of actions must not be allowed to impose organisational inertia. If there is a danger of this arising the factional impasse must be broken by the introduction of an external party that possesses the authority to select a direction and command the resources necessary to fuel the momentum of change.

5

The six stages of crisis
development

If the problems of turbulent times remain inadequately addressed and a real (as opposed to an illusory) bubble of stability is not created then managers tend to follow a consistent sequence of behavioural traits as the problems unfold and deteriorate into crises.

In summary, the sequence through which managers move is as follows:

1. Denial

2. Concealment

3. Containment

4. Negotiation

5. Confrontation

6. Collapse

The first three phases are concerned with controlling the sphere in which the problem is recognised. The last three phases arise when external assistance and support is necessary to address the problem.

The following figure illustrates how these phases relate to the T-matrix.

T-Matrix, including the six stages of crisis development

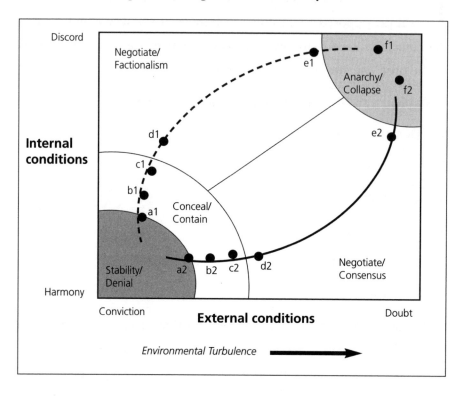

Key

a1	Contested denial	a2	Unified denial
b1	Contested concealment	b2	Weakly unified concealment
c1	Strongly opposed containment imposed by dominant faction	c2	Contested containment
d1	Negotiation with overt internal disagreement	d2	Negotiation without consensus
e1	Confrontation between factions and external stakeholders	e2	Confrontation with external stakeholders in a climate of weak internal discord
f1	Disintegration and collapse	f2	Disintegration and collapse

1. Denial

Denial begins at the point at which some long trend of stability ends and the shadows of unexpected outcomes become apparent but remain capable of another more benign explanation.

Sometimes there is general agreement amongst the management team that they can see no cause for concern (position a2) and in other organisations the notion of denial is disputed (position a1) but there is no policy change as, in the first case, no need is perceived and, in the second case, there is no consensus for change.

Most crises mature gradually but at an accelerating rate. By the time they migrate from a problem to a crisis in which a wider collection of parties must recognise their own exposure and vulnerability they move up a gear, turbulence leads to instability and panic and collapse becomes a significant risk.

There is an unfortunate tendency that, at an early stage, crisis management becomes a series of isolated insights floating on an ocean of generalisations. This is the consequence of inexperienced people with little direct expertise in crisis management attempting to create the impression that everything is under control.

Manufacturing this illusion by attempting misdirection, while understandable, does nothing to address the underlying issues, allows the position to deteriorate and destroys credibility. No one is fooled that, however elaborate the illusion, the magician can *really* make the elephant disappear.

Of the many variables in the complex equation some that have remained constant over the recent past begin to change, and others that have hitherto varied only slowly begin to accelerate. You may become uncertain about the relationship between cause and effect and a different psychology may be noticeable amongst your colleagues.

For example:

- Lenders become more stringent in analysing compliance with covenants and, as incidents of default increase, they become more diligent in evaluating loan renewals.

- The growth in consumer demand diminishes as the availability of credit declines.

- Inflation increases to reach a recent peak.

- Pressure grows for wage and salary increases in excess of previous levels and suppliers seek higher than usual price increases.

- Productivity gains become harder to achieve.

Investment in working capital grows faster than sales value or gross profit.

But, despite all the above, you argue that all this is manageable and doesn't necessarily signal the beginning of a deteriorating trend.

Many managers believe that acknowledgement of a possibility is self-fulfilling prophecy. If you admit that there *may* be a problem then this is a substantial step towards acceptance that there *is* a problem, and from this it is a short distance to the problem emerging seemingly because by acknowledging the possibility you induced the reality.

Governments take this position in the very late stages of the credit cycle when the probability of a turning point increases and a cyclical recessionary adjustment is likely. Because the government accounts for such a substantial fraction of the economy (certainly in Western states) it is logical to suppose that their pessimistic conclusions, if widely disseminated, will move markets and may cause a turning point equivalent to that which they predict may arise for other reasons.

When a recession is encountered the government is invariably criticised for maintaining the position of denial for too long, and often opposition politicians use this as evidence of the government's economic incompetence.

But few managers have this degree of economic power and their acceptance or denial of reality will not cause events. Nor can the thinking manager justify inaction by pointing to the government's optimism. Managerial denial is no more than deliberate self-deception, the psychological expression of fear of an unexpected event and an unpredictable future.

In this state of denial information that supports the assertion that there are no grounds for concern is given greater weight than reports of negative indicators. The latter are challenged, the credibility of the messenger questioned and the organisational elite begin to practice mutual reinforcement of their increasingly myopic if not delusional view of the world.

This is also the onset of anxiety in the form of emerging but repressed apprehension about possible developments that are growing in probability but, as yet, not entirely clear.

2. Concealment

When the internal evidence of deteriorating performance becomes too strong to be ignored or discredited it is concealed. The mantra becomes:

the problem and its consequences must be held confidential until plans can be formulated for a response that leads to its eradication.

Anxiety turns to fear as the threat is now apparent and the danger real and present. It is at this point when the cohesion of the previously united management team begins to disintegrate.

There are occasions when internal denial becomes unsustainable because the problem enters the public arena through a different channel beyond management's control and concealment takes the form of public denial of any deleterious effects.

In following the path of denial and concealment, management, in its attempt to impose control on the spreading of awareness of the problem, risks the problem becoming a crisis[9] by not taking overt action to address it in their desire to maintain the false impression that there is nothing to be concerned about. Politicians are past masters at falling into this trap.

On the T-matrix the organisation is now positioned at b1 or b2 and close to the threshold at which problems are visible in the public domain.

---

[9] I define a crisis as a significant problem that is generally acknowledged but for which there is no apparent solution.

The real risk lies in the ability of management to formulate a credible remedial plan so that when the issue enters the public arena, as it inevitably will, it does so in a positive light.

Yes, we have encountered a problem that, potentially, may have a detrimental effect on the organisation but, by recognising this at an early stage, management has been able to formulate plans to neutralise/minimise the worst effects and to protect the organisation from the consequences that would otherwise have occurred.

This a better story than:

Yes, we have encountered a problem that, potentially, may have a detrimental effect on the organisation but management is working hard to ascertain the extent of the problem and the possible effects it may have. Be assured that management is doing everything it can at this difficult time.

Why do managers deny and conceal the existence of serious problems?

I believe that the answer has much to do with the inflexibility of the system in which they operate.

There are both emotional and rational elements to be considered.

Emotional

Emotionally, managers recognise that the onset of some form of serious turbulence dislocates their established processes to the extent that they become potentially unreliable. To be left rudderless in the middle of a storm is the antithesis of scientific management.

Some managers fail to recognise that the methodologies on which they have come to depend are no longer trustworthy and persist in using them. This is when problems usually turn into crises. The following processes, I argue, become flawed:

Process	Problem
Strategic planning	Unpredictable operating conditions
Investment appraisal using DCF techniques	Unpredictable cost of available capital and cash flows
Forecasting based on time series analysis	Potential discontinuity
Competitor analysis based on previous performance	Unpredictable industry structure
Prediction of consumer demand based on performance during the previous year and used to underpin budgets	Market uncertainty

Let me also offer the possibility of deflation as a single devastating characteristic of a severe economic downturn that corrodes all the above.

Declining prices, in things other than food, petrol and other energy products, alter consumer psychology to the extent that they are inclined to defer purchases, especially discretionary purchases such as durables, in expectation of lower prices tomorrow to the extent that demand can collapse and all techniques dependent on the continuation of trends established in and assuming the continuation of a climate of inflation are invalidated.

There is no history to rely on as the economy is no longer paused but has entered a discontinuity.

Could such a thing occur in a modern market economy?

Well, it happened to Japan in the 1990s!

It arose in the US and UK housing markets in 2008, where falling housing prices led to those able to arrange mortgage finance being reluctant to proceed with transactions because tomorrow the price of the asset may decline further.

In concealment there is also the matter of self-esteem to be considered. A crisis reflects badly on the incumbent management. They may become slightly paranoid believing that if stakeholders become aware of the problems they will ask:

Did management predict problems? If not why?

If they predicted difficulties why did they not take action to ameliorate the effects?

Either way it seems that the admission of problems leads directly to personal criticism and questions about competency. Turbulence is seen to be a breakdown of management and therefore the failure of managers.

At this point corporate problems become a personal, professional risk.

If that is what unalloyed honesty attracts then it is understandable that some managers believe that the best course is to deny or bury the problem until either a solution can be formulated or an exit found that disassociates them from the problem! But this assumes that concealment is a rational process, whereas in most cases it is an emotional response following the inability to continue the self-delusion in the phase of denial.

How can this tendency be overcome?

Well, it is unlikely that the psychology will change as it is rooted in that most fundamental of behaviour; whether to fight or run when danger is perceived. That same instantaneous response to a potential threat that causes each of us to manufacture adrenalin.

Think of the way in which you experience metabolic changes when potentially serious problems are revealed. The tingling in the back of your hands and changes in your respiration. These are the symptoms of this fundamental response preparing you for an exceptional physical effort.

But, of course, in the arena we are concerned with, an immediate physical response is inappropriate. Where are you going to run to? With whom are you going to fight? In other words your evolutionary neurological response is no longer tuned to provide the appropriate emotional state required to confront this contemporary problem.

These, automatic, responses were developed to protect our ancient ancestors from physical, not abstract, threats to their wellbeing.

In modern turbulent times when you need the enhancement of your intellectual capabilities it is your physical attributes that are stimulated.

It is not easy to say to a manager, 'Ok, your brain is sending the wrong signal so just ignore it!' We find the ability to enter some transcendental state very difficult. More so when others around us are revealing the same evolutionary reactions and the personal drive to respond physically by running or fighting is magnified by the herd instinct.

Think of the times that the natural reaction to problems has been to call for immediate action, do something, don't just think about it, some conspicuous action is needed to demonstrate that you are motivated to deal with it. It almost doesn't matter that the action may be ineffective. Just run, it doesn't matter in which direction you escape, just go!

If you're going to fight, then just pick either the closest or weakest target and attack. Attacking may deter an adversary but if the threat is an economic recession how can you face this down? Well, that's exactly what governments appear to try by denying the onset of economic difficulties until they are unable to maintain a policy of denial and concealment any longer.

What can be done?

Get the matter into the open so that each member of your team comes to realise that you all share the same concerns.

In other words try to move down the vertical axis of the T-matrix to a position of greater harmony.

Don't think alone. Share your perspective with close colleagues. If you cannot do so then either you have problems with the people close to you or you have a problem with your own psychology. Additionally, involve someone who is not emotionally attached to the organisation and can therefore be wholly dispassionate.

That means do not rely exclusively on your independent directors and your regular advisers. They have an interest in preserving you as a client, which means they may be reluctant to advocate a path that is not in their interests or to criticise your instinctive conduct. Additionally, they have their own reputation to protect which may be linked to your performance. Finally, their own path of denial, concealment, etc., distorts their objectivity.

To consult someone who is not emotionally attached to you or your business sounds like a straightforward logical step. But in reality it takes a brave manager to recognise the risks to good judgement that are created by subjectivity and emotional responses. Exposing your concerns to a stranger is an additional challenge to be confronted at a time when your instinct is to internalise.

Choose your thinking partner carefully.

Meanwhile, there are other initiatives that you can take.

Have the organisation prepare operational plans on the optimistic basis while you and a few colleagues prepare the pessimistic view. The key is to have the wider organisation search for the positive information and actions while the negative positions are evaluated by a smaller group.

The methodology, philosophers call it a dialectic, is designed to interpose two opposing views in order to resolve the differences between them rather than to establish which one is true.

If someone puts the pessimistic view then debate the issues by having the pessimist argue the optimistic view and give someone who is optimistically inclined the task of advocating the pessimistic outlook. In other words if there are factions emerging force each of them into the territory of the other and see where that takes you, who changes their mind, which arguments are robust or weak, etc.

You are attempting to minimise the prejudicial positions reinforced by emotional responses by causing people to question their assumptions. You run because you think you see a lion. You relax because someone you trust tells you it is a trick of the light. You fight because someone rushes towards you with what appears to be a knife. You relax because someone steps forward and shows you that it's just a shiny umbrella.

The key is the intervention of another person who is unaffected by the emotional response you and your colleagues experience and who can change your psychological state by revealing that there is no problem or, if there is, they help you to gain clarity and to respond rationally.

Rational

Rationally, managers may believe that by revealing problems to potentially effected parties (who themselves recognise their limited options and therefore the attraction of grabbing what they can as first in the queue) they will simply precipitate the destabilisation they wish to avoid.

Indeed, at the emotional level, these potentially disadvantaged third parties also wish to avoid the recognition of your problems.

In part the rational process is an attempt to formulate an objective prediction of the emotional reaction of affected parties.

It is often said that a company should inform its bankers at the earliest opportunity of concerns that may change the basis of the bank's understanding of the business. The implication is that the bank has some benign means of addressing actual or potential corporate difficulty if they are informed at an early stage. The reality is different. The earlier they learn of problems the greater the time available to assess their position. Experience informs them that the sooner they act the greater the value of their collateral.

One, perhaps the main, motivation of managers in concealing emerging problems is the rational decision to acquire the greatest possible time in the hope that either the problems can be avoided or rectified and will not need to be shared. Or when the moment comes when they can be concealed no longer, the presentation of the problems can be accompanied by a coherent solution.

Of course, those who are potentially disadvantaged by the problems, like lenders, would, if they were aware, regard this conduct as prejudicing their interests by denying them their preferred timescale.

In concealing the magnitude of problems managers are taking action (even the consumption of time) that causes other options to be eliminated, and if subsequently the problem can no longer be concealed the actual position is closer to a crisis as the other options have been permanently eliminated.

Hence concealment that is not accompanied by remedial action makes worse the problem and therefore lessens the chance of keeping the event out of the public arena. But the implementation of remedial action tends to put the problems in the public domain thereby drawing attention to management's earlier concealment.

In anticipation of this behaviour stakeholders often impose seemingly onerous (less trusting) obligations at the outset to protect their interests. These covenants to inform convince managers that if a problem emerges the stakeholders (most usually a bank, bond holder or private equity investor) will exercise their rights immediately they learn of the difficulties facing the company. This, in turn, leads management to conceal any problems which potentially could trigger action under these covenants.

How can this unwanted circle be interrupted? Here is an example:

In late 2008, Premier Foods PLC had net debt of GBP 1.8bn and a market worth of under GBP 200mm. This was the financial aftermath of a series of acquisitions culminating in the purchase of RHM in 2007.

The banks lending to the company were due to receive a covenant stress test of Premier Food's balance sheet as at 31st December 2008, but Premier negotiated an agreement with the syndicate that the test would be postponed until 31st March 2009 in return for a payment of GBP 4.9mm.

The reasoning was that conducting the test was pointless because Premier was in the process of renegotiating the shape of this debt and anticipated that this would be concluded by 31st March 2009. Hence, if the covenants were breached, which Premier asserted they were confident would not be the case, the banks would be placed in the difficult position of either deciding to do nothing and allow the debt restructuring discussions to continue, which was the status quo. Or the banks could take action to reclaim their security in a particularly unattractive market for selling distressed assets thereby bringing the refinancing discussions to a premature end and probably prejudicing their own level of recovery. What was to be lost by postponing the test? From the point of view of the banks, probably very little.

This example reveals how, by searching for the intersection of all party's interests, a stable bubble of time can be created in which a more robust realignment of interests can be sought.

Of course by putting this arrangement in the public domain Premier raised the stakes in the refinancing negotiations. Potential lenders became aware that time is of the essence and existing lenders became concerned about what action to take if their exposure remains and the covenants are broken.

In the almost unprecedented credit market of early 2009 Premier gambled on the likelihood that most of its existing banks would recognise the futility of trying to attract replacement lenders and renew their facilities at higher margins but also with a new set of more extensive covenants that reflect Premier's changed financial and operating position. In such conditions conducting an appraisal on the basis of the 'old' covenants appears meaningless.

Trust

A significant cause of management's concealment of problems is a lack of trust.

Much has been written about the degree of trust that is necessary or present in modern commercial relationships, but one of the clear effects of turbulent times is their corrosive effect on the level of trust throughout the system.

Employees no longer trust managers to protect their livelihood and shareholders believe that no-one will place their interests at the front of the line. For example, if a lender trusted a borrower to repay they would not require collateral to be pledged and certainly not the provisions enabling intervention enshrined in the loan documentation.

In 2008, banks even stopped trusting each other and interbank lending virtually ceased. It then becomes a stretch of credibility for the banks to suggest that borrowers should trust them when they distrust each other.

Trust is something that is easily broken but cannot be repaired as effortlessly. But re-establishing trust is necessary to the calming of economic turbulence. Although it is mutually desirable it re-emerges comparatively slowly and tentatively, and while governments can introduce fiscal stimuli to restart economic activity they find it difficult to rekindle trust and must be content with attempting to compensate for its absence.

3. Containment

Only when the pattern of decline is too apparent to be concealed does a new urgency arise in the identification of a reliable defensive posture. Managers may fear that this will be misinterpreted as panic and that a crisis mentality may become established.

At this stage managers can be drawn into a policy of containment. They realise that the difficulties cannot be resolved without widening the circle of those aware of the problem in detail, but are concerned to ensure that this enlargement of those 'in the know' doesn't extend to full exposure in the public domain.

The general view is often that the changes that are now unavoidable will be conspicuous and hence the problem that motivated the action will be apparent, but the wider audience will be able to apprehend both a problem and its solution and that is preferable to the current situation where there is the acknowledgement of a problem but no solution.

This is a rather idealistic phase that usually has a comparatively short duration as it is almost impossible to prevent the closed circle of awareness from leaking information. Of course, in public companies directors have an obligation to inform the market of any material adverse change in the company's prospects that, if concealed, would lead to a false market.

Trying to preserve a state of concealment in order to avoid the almost impossible objective of containment simply leads to the immobilisation of the company. No action can be taken that may alert a wider audience to the nature of the problems and therefore to management's less than positive psychology. This can only mean that no action or inadequate action will become the prevailing policy which, in turn, will allow the problem to become a crisis and explode into the public domain in an uncontrolled way.

Turning again to the T-matrix, it is at this point that a company that is following the lower of the two trajectories can jump to the upper line as the cohesion of the management team disintegrates to be replaced by factional disagreement.

Containment is never more than a brief interlude between the failure of concealment and the onset of negotiation.

4. Negotiation

We have now reached the phase at which concealment is no longer an option, either because the organisation cannot avoid admission of the difficulties it faces even though it has no credible plan to deal with them, or because there is a plan but it cannot be implemented covertly or perhaps additional resources, usually financial, may be required to 'buy' the time and fund the costs associated with the action that is proposed.

On the T-matrix the company has moved into the corridor of uncertainty at point d1 or d2.

Management must now embark on a process of dialogue and negotiation with stakeholders and potential stakeholders in order to advise them of the consequences of inaction and the cost of action. Note that to existing stakeholders the proposition is not expressed in terms of marginal reward to additional investment risk but as the cost of protecting what will otherwise be lost.

In many cases, especially those that need additional funding, this conversation takes the form of:

Do nothing and everything you have may be lost.

Take an additional risk and you will not only protect what you have but will make additional gains.

If you reduce it to its fundamental components this is an attempt at coercion. The undisguised attempt to extract additional resources under threat.

To potential stakeholders the proposition is presented as an opportunity to take over the position of reluctant existing stakeholders who have declined the opportunity to protect their investment. Put in these terms neither proposition is attractive.

The reaction to this is never enthusiastic and not always or often compliant. More often remedial plans are regarded with greater scepticism than the original investment decision. Management must overcome the doubt in their competence which inevitably accompanies any group who enter negotiations not saying that they have a great idea that will make a substantial return on the capital invested, but admitting that they have presided over a business they declared was in good shape only to have to 'beg' for additional support to overcome a difficulty they could not manage or avoid.

In 2008, the banking sector in all parts of the world provided the perfect example of these first four phases. Denial, concealment and attempts at containment were all obvious to anyone who watched the problems unfold. The eventual need to seek additional resources urgently to avoid collapse reveals just how few options remained when the problems the banks confronted leaked into the public arena.

Was there an alternative story in which the financial crisis could have been avoided?

I argue the answer is yes.

Of course the banks might have taken a more prudent stance towards building their exposure by not accepting sub prime risk and its derivatives. Regulators might have been more sanguine about the concept that risk could be managed through derivative instruments.

But the cyclical adjustment (recession in other words) that should have occurred around 2001/02 and might have exposed and moderated this practice was artificially avoided. How was this accomplished?

There is a reasonably robust argument that the origin of the 2008 problem occurred in 1998 when the US Federal Reserve decided to engineer a bail out of the failing hedge fund Long-Term Capital Management (LTCM). This action sent a signal to the US financial markets that elevated levels of risk could be taken almost with impunity.

The second critical decision was the Fed's decision to respond to declines in the US stock market by reducing interest rates to stimulate asset prices and thereby avoid a deflationary trend emerging.

The combined result was the capacity for asset bubbles to form and the avoidance of the cyclical adjustment due around 2001/02.

The dotcom bubble ended but failed to precipitate a widespread adjustment and was replaced by the larger domestic real estate bubble. This artificial extension of the credit cycle should have alerted all the players that the credit market was entering unknown territory and they should not have denied the increased probability of a sudden and severe adjustment.

Extending the credit cycle was an example of running a complex interconnected system beyond its specified limits for a period longer than it could tolerate. That the system reacted with a catastrophic collapse should not be surprising. There is always a limit. But this is a ridiculous and dangerous way to locate it! It is analogous to pretending that an activated nuclear weapon is not going to explode because you cannot see the countdown clock.

Banks (whether encouraged by their regulators or not) could have moderated their market activity had their management recognised the consequences of maintaining their business model at maximum torque and the heat could have been let out of the system gradually. There would still have been a recession in 2008, it was necessary and overdue, but probably milder and shorter than the alarmingly turbulent event being experienced as I write.

The turbulence would have been less and the capacity to manage through it successfully would have been proportionately greater.

The deeper and more widespread the turbulence the less chance there is for any but the most robust remedial plans to be underwritten by new resources. In this case there are two options for management to consider:

1. Struggle on and try to salvage something using the resources available.

    This is not always a freely available option as, in the process of negotiation, management has declared to stakeholders, including secured lenders, that without new resources the collapse of the company is the likely outcome.

    Consequently, lenders who tend to the view that in such circumstances their first loss is their smallest may call for repayment of their loans, which have entered a new risk category and are in breach of the loan documentation on the basis of anticipatory default.

    As a result there may be a brief interlude of confrontation (the next phase) but control has effectively passed from management's hands and the continuation of the company is dependent on the tolerance of lenders holding charges over assets.

2. Recognise that the company is probably insolvent and seek immediate protection under the particular bankruptcy law that has jurisdiction.

    Sometimes the bankruptcy law can be used in a positive way to facilitate a reorganisation that is not otherwise feasible. These are called pre-packaged bankruptcies because the outcome has been agreed before the company files for protection under the bankruptcy code.

Adopting a policy of negotiation can arise both prior to and following confrontation. The military example provides the clearest illustration when one of two parties engaged in conflict seeks a negotiated cessation of hostilities.

There are also good examples of this behaviour from the political arena. In 1940, Neville Chamberlain was Prime Minister of the United Kingdom. He had employed his not inconsiderable diplomatic skills to avert war with Nazi Germany but had failed and the UK was confronting the real threat of invasion.

The choice was simple:

1. Carry on and hope for the best

2. Seek some negotiated peace that may salvage something.

3. Change strategy and adopt a defiant stance that united the population in a final desperate attempt to acquire sufficient time to address the imbalance in military resources.

The choice was made to reject negotiation in favour of continued confrontation by taking what many thought the riskiest strategy of replacing Chamberlain with the charismatic but unpredictable Winston Churchill. It was by no means a unanimous decision but history reveals that it proved to be the decision that secured the continued independence of the UK.

Saddam Hussein appeared to pursue the 'carry on and hope for the best' option in his confrontation with the United States in 2002/3 by putting faith in the negotiating capacity of the United Nations to placate the aggressive stance taken by the US. It was the wrong choice and Saddam lost his position of power and ultimately his life.

When these choices are considered is usually the moment when incumbent management departs, as Chamberlain did, and not always voluntarily.

Negotiation underlines the disagreement between stakeholders and the need to find a new consensus.

If a cogent plan is presented that stakeholders believe to be in their interests then they may make the availability of new resources and further time conditional on the replacement of the management they now regard as discredited or not equipped to deal with the challenges.

Occasionally, managers find relief in the decision and problem being taken out of their hands.

5. Confrontation

On the T-matrix we have now moved more deeply into the corridor of uncertainty. Discord increases and, as earlier measures have not yielded the intended results, uncertainty grows and confidence declines.

Those managers who survive into the period of negotiation and have presided over the previous stages of the lifespan often become unable to function effectively in this turbulent phase as their record is one of denial, concealment and the failure of initiatives. If they lack credibility amongst those whose welfare is linked to the organisation they may not be trusted with directing the necessary changes to escape the current perilous position.

If they do continue in position they will be monitored regularly, extensively and more closely than ever before by stakeholders and their advisers.

But that is not the entire story.

Remedial plans that proceeded as a result of a successful negotiation phase and the acquisition of new resources often fail to deliver their intended output in the timescale envisaged.

This occurs in a significant fraction of cases because, in their desire for approval, incumbent management tends to underestimate the resources and the time required and overestimate the potential benefits.

Perhaps the general situation worsened unexpectedly or an unanticipated event, such as the collapse of a customer, created a revenue gap and an uninsured bad debt. Management may just have been unrealistically optimistic in their desperation to present a plan that offered the maximum performance for the minimum investment.

The consequence is a confrontation between management, established stakeholders and especially new funders. The latter are usually the most strident in accusing management of incompetence; even new managers introduced at the negotiation phase are not immune to criticism.

Management usually replies that the plan was sound given the situation that prevailed at the time and if they could be given a few more months of stability then everything will turn out OK.

Given the difficulty in acquiring new resources and a bubble of stability during the negotiation phase, this request for indulgence is a very difficult call that rarely meets with success if the incumbent and probably discordant management team are to remain in place. Usually this is the point at which they are asked to step aside to allow specialist turnaround managers to take control.

There is little time remaining and few resources, and this move is often the last resort to avoid collapse.

The new team will probably make acceptance of the assignment conditional upon:

- The availability of the funds denied to the departing discredited management.

- A binding standstill agreement with major creditors, bondholders and lenders to provide a platform of stability for the next few months.

In conditions of political turbulence the same stage is reached when the failure of diplomatic relations is followed by an outbreak of hostilities.

It is unusual for all the parties who were prominent in the failed diplomatic activity to be able to broker the avoidance of hostilities.

A ceasefire can sometimes be arranged by the intervention of a new peacekeeping force that holds the current position while a durable plan for peace is formulated in a climate in which the hostile parties are disengaged from management of the problem.

In too many cases this change of management takes place too late in the sequence of deterioration. Ideally, the managerial change to someone with specialist experience and the ability to operate in turbulent times should take place as a condition of a successful negotiation about remedial plans and new resources and not when this plan has failed. But stakeholders often remain convinced that company and industry knowledge trumps remedial management skill.

This illogical notion is not supported by evidence. It does not follow that industry knowledge brings experience or ability of managing through turbulent times. It is situational capability that is necessary.

At this stage the company is either stabilised, sold or deteriorates further, leading to collapse.

6. Collapse

In this final phase the organisation is no longer viable. The consequences of this are:

- Its break up and sale of the assets usually at a heavy discount to their book value.

- Its forced merger with competitors who may also be encountering problems but not of the same magnitude, and it is believed that the creation of a larger entity will produce a viable organisation that may preserve the value of all the assets.

- In the political arena the requesting of assistance from the IMF who will impose a management solution on the elected government or surrender to and occupation by a superior force.

In most cases collapse into bankruptcy is not entirely attributable to the assets in question being non-viable. It is mostly a technical device for separating an intransigent and failed management from the assets so that they can be transferred without obstruction into the hands of a third party.

To illustrate how the stages of crisis development apply generally I have compared a summary of the progression from denial through to collapse in the gestation of the failure of the US bank Lehman Brothers in 2008 and the second Iraq war in 2003 as seen from the Iraqi perspective.

	Lehman	Iraq
Denial	Lehman Brothers became highly exposed to the real estate market during the final phase of the credit cycle and, particularly, became a dominant force in the US sub-prime mortgage market. At the end of 2006 Mike Gelband, Lehman's head of commercial and residential real estate, believed that this sector had reached its peak and that the bank needed a new business model. Lehman's CEO, the pugnacious Dick Fuld, argued that Gelband was too conservative and wrong. He persisted and by mid-2007 Gelband had been fired.	The US accuses Iraq of the covert manufacture of weapons of mass destruction (WMD). The Iraqi government rejects this allegation but the real denial is that this initial act is an act of defiance that will have catastrophic consequences which, at this stage, could have been avoided by adopting a different strategy.
Concealment	Lehman reported a reduced first quarter 2008 profit while competitors such as Merrill and Citi reported losses of $1.97bn and $5.1bn respectively. But this attracted comment that the profit had been engineered by overvaluing assets and recognising unrepeatable profit. When the new CFO, Erin Callan, was asked by CNBC whether Lehman would follow Bear Stearns and require a bail out she replied 'categorically no!' On 9 June Lehman reported a second quarter loss of $2.8bn and a $6bn capital raising.	The Iraqi authorities impede access of weapons inspectors appointed by the UN to various suspect installations and fail to provide a convincing explanation for satellite photographs of possible WMD facilities. This is perceived by the US and its allies as evidence of a policy of concealment. It may have been so.

	Lehman	Iraq
Containment	After reporting the loss Fuld began an increasingly regular dialogue with US Treasury Secretary Paulson. Internally it has been reported that Fuld would not tolerate any negative information and that the senior management became increasingly introverted, hardly communicating outside their closed circle.	As a consequence of the failure of the problem to be rectified in phases I and II, the Iraqi government sought to contain the growing problem within the diplomatic arena in which complex protocols could be developed to diffuse the bellicose US administration while at the same time preserving the integrity of the Iraqi regime under Saddam Hussein.
Negotiation	By mid-June 2008 CFO Callan had been forced out and a new President, Herb McDade, had relieved Fuld of much executive power. McDade's more analytical method revealed the extent of Lehman's problems and so began a summer long, increasingly desperate, programme of seeking a buyer.	When containment failed and economic sanctions began to impoverish the state, the Iraqi government attempted to negotiate a settlement that allowed it to remain in power.
Confrontation	On 9 September J.P. Morgan asked Lehman to deposit a further $5bn of collateral in cash otherwise it could not open Lehman's account on the following day and would freeze their accounts. No cash was available. On 10 September Lehman announced a loss of $3.9bn and alarm bells began to ring around Wall St.	Iraqi's principal adversary was the USA who, while not wishing to instigate unilateral action was impatient with the 'soft' diplomacy of the UN. They provoked a confrontation with increasingly strident demands for total compliance by Iraq to demands for unimpeded access to any and every facility in their territory. The Iraqi regime argued that the aggression of the US was unreasonable but they failed to understand that the US wanted a resolution and not a procedure and that progression from one phase to the next was irreversible.

	Lehman	**Iraq**
Collapse	Lehman thought a deal could be concluded with Barclays and due diligence commenced only for Barclays to inform them that any transaction was subject to shareholder approval which would take some weeks to acquire. The deal was off; Lehman ran out of time and on 15 September filed for bankruptcy.	The USA and its allies made a final demand that the obdurate regime of Saddam Hussein should remove itself from power within days. Failure to comply would trigger military action to remove them and expose their duplicity regarding WMDs. The consequence was that the Ba'ath party regime of Saddam Hussein was removed militarily, Iraq was occupied and entered a prolonged period of civil turbulence that continues 5 years after the initial military action ended. Importantly, no WMDs have been discovered.

In the Lehman case Bryan Marsal, the co-CEO of Alvarez and Marsal, the firm appointed to restructure Lehman said:

> '...this bankruptcy...occurred with no planning. Had the rules of crisis management been followed much of the value that was lost by the unsecured creditors [c. $180bn out of a total of c. $200bn] would have been prevented.'

The Cuban Missile Crisis of 1962 provides another good example but in this case collapse – an exchange of nuclear weapons between the USA and USSR – was averted only when both parties modified their strategy at the confrontation stage with the realisation that only one stage remained and that it was in the interests of neither party to go there.

Using the T-matrix to map these cases the following conclusions may be drawn:

1. In the example of Lehman, discord grew within the management team as the dominant and autocratic CEO persisted with the denial that a problem existed and then with the delusion that 'the zero option', by which he meant the collapse into bankruptcy, was inconceivable.

    Lehman failed to confront the severity of their problems until the deterioration had become too great and the remedy too urgent to be facilitated by the action that was possible in the time remaining.

    Lehman moved inexorably along both axes of the T-matrix while believing themselves invulnerable. They accelerated along the top line into zone E and collapsed.

2. Saddam Hussein was also unable to prevent discord emerging between his regime and his principal adversary (the US regime of George W. Bush). Neither party invested sufficiently in trying to relieve the other's mistrust and doubt. As trust was minimal Iraq drifted into zone E and collapsed.

3. In the Cuban Missile Crisis the resolution was found late into the confrontation phase. By reducing the level of discord and thereby moving both parties down the vertical axis from their positions in zone C to zone B.

The important lesson is that managing the individual phases rather than the system of deterioration as a whole can lead to disaster. The objective of doing so is clear: to try and arrest the problem at an early stage before it becomes a crisis. But few realise that by focussing on the current stage without understanding the sequence as a whole is a significant contributory factor in continued deterioration.

Managing through turbulent times is not a *project* but a *process*.

From these examples it is also apparent that, if you fail to understand and to manage your adversary's agenda and rely only on promoting your own position, you run the risk of failing to regain control over the path both you and they will be obliged to travel by the force of the turbulence that surrounds you.

Turbulent times seem to impose their own momentum on events and the psychology of the participants, as often multiple problems seem to arise in close succession. At times it may seem as if the turbulence has a metaphysical guiding mind intent on driving the organisation towards a catastrophic outcome.

It is the manifestation of the force that pushes all organised systems towards disorder unless they are maintained with vigilance in a stable state.

When the paths taken by organisations that collapsed and states that have gone to war are examined, the analysis reveals points at which such a catastrophic outcome could have been avoided but a different course was chosen. It appears that reason becomes subordinated to some other decision-making process that is not entirely emotional.

Management observing the commencement of turbulence and now cognisant of the above phases need to be aware of this last statement. There is usually a solution. In the last resort it may not be to your liking but, had this been adopted at an earlier stage by you taking a more realistic attitude about the limited prospects of preserving the assets and structure to which you have become emotionally attached, the company may not have been damaged to the extent that intensive care and emergency multiple amputation of assets was the only course remaining.

Psychology militates against incumbent management adopting this radical position or indeed any radical position at an early stage as they seek the minimum possible disruption to their established programmes consistent with survival.

But often the pace of destabilisation in turbulent times is faster than management's capacity to exert control in the orthodox way and the result is the implementation of a series of gradually more extensive remedial plans, each of which reacts to the deterioration observed to date and rarely to that projected by the trend.

When managers are reactionary their action tends to be slightly out of phase with the growing problem and is therefore insufficiently effective. It is the application of yesterday's solution to tomorrow's problem.

I believe that the crucial starting point is to recognise and admit that a problem exists. When the general economic environment is turbulent it is unreasonable to assume without compelling evidence that your company will escape without a negative impact.

If you recognise the symptoms of denial in yourself or your colleagues or if you notice a growing irreconcilable disagreement amongst your team (i.e. moving up the vertical axis of the T-matrix) you should regard this as an important warning signal and appreciate from the above discussion where it might lead.

6

The effect of turbulent times

Generally speaking, in a recession in which the UK economy contracts by up to 3%, around 3% of businesses collapse. Most, but not all, of these are SMEs.

Only c.15% of businesses pass through the period of general turbulence unscathed and few of these prosper.

That leaves around 80% of businesses that encounter some negative impact.

Some of these companies will be damaged but emerge able to take advantage of the resumption of growth, others will emerge damaged and function as the corporate disabled for many years following the turbulent phase until they are acquired by a stronger competitor or fail as a result of their inability to withstand a further shock.

In summary these are the broad categories:

	Approx % of businesses	Description	Examples
Resistant	15%	Businesses that are unaffected or suffer minimal affects and able to preserve their structure and processes unchanged.	Utilities A&E medical
Healthy Survivors	82%	Businesses that encounter problems but have the resources and flexibility to resolve them by refinancing and restructuring. Those that act quickly and do not deny or conceal their problems. Those with low leverage.	Banks (usually) Defence contractors Public transport Top 4 food retailers Energy companies
Disabled Survivors		Businesses that deny and conceal the problems they eventually cannot ignore. As a result they incur more damage by delaying remedial action.	Private equity deals completed during the previous two years Furniture companies Car manufacturers and distributors
Defenceless	3%	High fixed-cost businesses Recently formed businesses Highly leveraged consumer-facing Businesses, intermediaries and agents	High volume, low margin retailers Road haulage Hotels Builders and civil engineers Real estate companies

The Defenceless

For some companies their business model and balance sheet weakness combine to condemn them to failure. They tend to fail during the early stages of turbulence and the pace of their collapse is such that management can do little to arrest the decline. They have no corporate immune system.

Their decline from denial to collapse tends to take less than 12 months.

The Resistant

Resilient businesses include those perceived, and maybe even criticised during the final stages of the credit cycle, to have been unadventurous in that they did not use cheap, covenant-lite lending to acquire other companies at substantial premia, finance share repurchase or dividend enhancement. Their reticence has, however, enabled them to enter the turbulence with a comparatively strong balance sheet. In particular, the company is not characterised by the destabilising weakness of high leverage that cannot be refinanced thereby rendering the company vulnerable to the changing sentiment or instability of a lender.

These are companies that have a surfeit of resources and an unimpaired corporate immune system.

The UK bank Lloyds TSB is a good example. It didn't embrace the cutting edge financial and derivative products with the enthusiasm of its competitors RBS and HBOS. Once it was thought to be vulnerable to acquisition by a more aggressive institution as it had a balance sheet that was capable of greater leverage, but its moderation provided stability when the financial crisis struck in 2008 to the extent that it became the safe haven for the then unstable HBOS which Lloyds TSB acquired at a discount.

* * * *

The dominant categories contain the 80% of businesses that will survive. They will not avoid the destabilising impact of the economic turbulence and a significant number will perform sub-optimally for many years after the turbulence ends.

These are the categories in which managerial action or inaction in turbulent times is necessary and most effective.

Healthy Survivors

Companies that possess a reasonable degree of immunity to the economic contagion have a resilience that is easily squandered or lost unless it is secured at an early stage.

The typical features that suggest this resilience are:

- A dominant position in their market (#1 with a share in excess of 30%)

- No single customer accounts for more than 10% of revenue – so their capacity to absorb the loss of a major customer will be higher than average

- EBIT > 20% of cost of goods sold (COGS) – so that the company can absorb reasonable cost of goods increases and a fall in market volume without becoming unprofitable

- EBIT > 10% of GP (Gross Profit) – otherwise the operational gearing is probably unsustainable if revenue and GP decline. In other words the business model is dependant on stable conditions

- Debt: equity < 50%

These are only general indicators of resilience. A company that possesses all these characteristics is likely to be more resilient than one that has none. But nothing is guaranteed and managerial complacency can erode every advantage more rapidly in turbulent times than in stable conditions.

The principal danger is complacency when a strong position encourages managers to deny problems not because they fear them but because they are overconfident about their resilience.

I would counsel caution to managers running a company in such an enviable position because turbulence is rarely spread evenly across the economy and if their sector suffers disproportionately there is a level of contraction that will hurt them. The frequently heard comment that competitors will collapse first and we will benefit from their customers is logical but never certain, as other competitors will be desperate to win this marginal business and may force down your margins in their anxiety.

Managers who are accustomed to operating in unchallenging conditions are usually poorly equipped psychologically to deal with significant reversals and often respond inadequately and too late, as the pace of decline can outstrip their capacity to instigate a considered response. To use an athletics analogy, they are like weightlifters (big, strong, durable) who are suddenly asked to compete in a 400m hurdle race (where speed, energy management and competitive positioning are key). It is not their discipline and their training and experience does not equip them to compete.

Healthy survivors tend to be businesses for which demand is not sensitive to economic contraction; utilities are good examples. Consumer demand for utilities tends to be resilient as households cut back on discretionary expenditure to pay their mortgage, food and utility bills. Large businesses that are sensitive to industrial consumption may see sales volume decline somewhat, but often high volumes are acquired at fine margins and the small reduction in gross profit that result from the larger percentage reduction in sales is usually manageable.

Companies that fall into this survival group are usually run by managers who recognised the onset of potential problems at an early stage, usually well before the formal declaration of recession.

They did not deny the possibility or attempt to conceal the early signs of problems but acted immediately to restructure and to maximise the flexibility and adaptability of their company. They reduced the number of investment projects in assets and new products. Loans due to mature within the next two years were refinanced immediately. Unused facilities were drawn in full to avoid their cancellation.

Disabled Survivors

Also falling into this survival category are those business that are not able to restructure their company fully and/or adopt a new business model that will increase their competitive fitness when conditions improve but nonetheless are able to survive.

These businesses encounter problems, survive into the stable period that inevitably follows turbulence, but are damaged by the experience to an extent that impairs their ability to function with the same effectiveness that they enjoyed prior to encountering difficulties.

Their corporate immune system was only just adequate and may have required external support; the consequence of which is that they suffer an enduring deficiency that cannot be resolved simply.

Managers are human and are programmed to respond to threatening situations by preferring survival, even if it can be achieved only at the cost of disability.

So, the management of these businesses often subscribe to the notion that in turbulent times you must do whatever it takes to survive until the operating environment improves and then consider the options available to rectify or compensate for the disability.

It is the pragmatic abandonment of strategy and its replacement by a sequence of tactics.

I suggest that if you cannot conceive of a satisfactory solution to the problems that confront you it is rational to defer the need for action for as long as possible in the hope that better solutions will emerge, but managing the time pressure must not be mistaken for managing the problems. Remember the example given earlier of Saddam Hussein's misconceived strategy in the run-up to the Iraq war of 2003.

This is a clear signal of inept management. In these cases it is vital for independent directors or powerful stakeholders to recognise the deficiency and to engineer the earliest possible replacement of incumbent senior management by new people with different capabilities and a new mindset.

Often, management whose ineptitude is exposed by turbulent times may have been capable during the preceding stages of growth and stability. Generally, we make the mistake of imagining that competent managers are not situation specific but ought to be capable of dealing with all conditions. The history of corporate distress has revealed this to be a fallacy but it remains a notion that we cling to, making it more difficult to remove a senior manager who cannot cope with an unexpected situation until he or she has demonstrated conspicuous failure.

I have heard this likened this to a patient who has a heart attack in the dentist's chair and his dependent family saying: *let the dentist try to perform bypass surgery as he is the closest person with some medical knowledge*. The wrong knowledge but the right clothes is a dangerous combination. It is a powerful analogy and seems to apply in the Lehman example in which Dick Fuld had been an exceptional CEO in building the bank and delivering over 50 consecutive quarters of positive earnings. The attributes that enabled him to manage the business so effectively in this buoyant climate ceased to be effective in the brief but rapid phase in which turbulence struck.

In turbulent times one of the great risks is to be exposed to a business that is run by reactionary management and poorly informed stakeholders.

There is no doubt that it is better to survive than it is to collapse into failure and, if you are able to survive, it is preferable to be a healthy survivor and not a disabled survivor.

If we accept that to survive the organisation must possess structural characteristics that make it comparatively robust then the distinction between surviving healthily or with disability can be attributed to the action of management.

The structural benefits can be squandered by poor decisions, indecisiveness and the arrogant denial of vulnerability.

Some managers are not equipped to deal effectively with conditions of turbulence. In part because they may fail to recognise the onset of turbulent times but more often because they are allowed to direct the organisation in a situation that was never envisaged when they were recruited and their competency appraised.

This does not mean that they are deficient managers. It simply indicates that the prevailing circumstances require a skill set and experience that they do not possess.

* * * *

There are some important lessons that can be emphasised at this stage. They are:

- Take big decisions early.

- Change recalcitrant or inept management at an early stage.

- Be wary of businesses that were the subject of private equity deals late in the credit cycle (say two years before the commencement of the downturn in the economy). Their capital structure probably makes then vulnerable to financial distress.

- Also be wary of businesses run by recently acquisitive management who have gambled their reputation on earnings growth from the integration of acquired businesses. Especially those that have funded deals predominantly with debt containing covenants referring to asset disposals or liquidity ratios.

No-one can be certain about what challenges turbulent times will set for them and consequently implanting and preserving flexibility is not just desirable but essential.

- Treat with caution those companies with managers who exude conviction about the potential for success of a single plan. Unshakeable commitment to a single plan can be fatal. Only those able to lead with ingenuity, able to formulate creative options and to act with the courage to abandon previously favoured plans and projects will see their company emerge with the strength to prosper.

What can be done?

Turbulence of growth

The psychology of the change from infancy to growth is the anticipation of 'becoming'. The phase in which the organisation struggles to become established, and raise capital. The early crisis of slower than expected acceptance into the marketplace has ended and the growth in demand that is now being experienced is validation of the organisation's acceptance by its customers. These are exciting times for which managers have no comparable historical data from which they can draw conclusions about trends and make projections. This is sometimes called the 'blue sky phase' because the managerial perspective is optimistic as they move in the general direction of their expectation of success.

The phase is turbulent because growth usually strains the organisation's resources. The capital required to invest in people, systems, accommodation and marketing is often not available prior to the demonstration that infancy has turned into growth, or if it is available it has probably not been committed in anticipation of this point of inflexion in the lifespan graph.

So the organisation is more than likely chasing its tail as growth exceeds its capacity to cope efficiently, and it must ensure that its success isn't short-lived because it is unable to deliver on its promises and customers become dissatisfied and fail to repeat their demand for products and services.

At the same time some of the limited and overstretched capacity must be devoted to finding new resources and to designing and establishing new systems and procedures.

The time lag between the availability of these new resources and the need for them can lead to crisis as inadequate systems are run beyond their maximum capacity.

If you run any system at or beyond its optimum operating level for too long it will collapse and the more complex it is the less time you can operate at this hyper level until it fails.

Turbulence of decline

The psychology associated with the change from maturity to decline is the opposite of that familiar to managers during the change from infancy to growth.

When the signs of decline are apparent managers become anxious and seek to recover a previous state when they were seemingly in control of a stable and predictable situation. They cannot see a desirable way forward and so they chose to reverse.

There are many analogies that can be used to describe the managerial psychology at this phase transition. The most dramatic is; what would you think and feel were you to be sliding off the edge of a cliff?

You know that if you continue to slide then you will accelerate uncontrollably to your death. Of course your instinct is to avoid this. So what are the options?

1. If you cry for help someone might come along and rescue you, but there is the risk that no-one hears or that your cries are ignored.

2. In case no-one hears you then your best option is to try and scramble back onto the stable, level ground on which you were situated before the slide began.

3. If '2' isn't feasible, can you slide down to some lower level (a ledge) at which your descent will be halted and at which you can re-evaluate your plight from a semi-secure position?

4. If none of the above are possible then you become resigned to your fate.

Put in this stark analogous way there do not seem to be many options available to the manager encountering decline.

There are some interesting economics arguments related to this. If a rescuer comes along and you have no other option you will pay whatever is demanded to haul you back to stable ground.

This is what happened in the banking crisis of 2008. Banks such as Merrill Lynch, HBOS, and RBS accepted whatever terms were offered to prevent their collapse. The urgency with which such decisions had to be taken was revealed by the collapse of Lehman Brothers. Over the weekend preceding the collapse talks were underway with Barclays and Bank of America to drag Lehman back from the edge of the cliff only for there to be no agreement and, by Monday, Lehman fell to its death.

Remedial action is usually associated with attempts to rectify conspicuous decline often following the crisis point at which other initiatives have been ineffective and the fear of collapse has distorted management psychology. Emotion begins to dominate reason and panic replaces moderation. To understand an individual's psychology in such situations we need look no further than the disorder that often accompanies the instruction to abandon ship. It is to avoid such chaos that the crew insist that their passengers rehearse crisis procedures. Companies tend not to conduct such rehearsals and therefore have few protocols for handling crises.

But before this point is reached there is often an attempt to return the organisation to its previous state in which performance was acceptable.

'Let's get back to basics' is the mantra heard in many boardrooms at this point. But this is misguided. The past is another country and the conditions in which the organisation succeeded cannot normally be re-established. The attempt to follow this intuitive appealing path is akin to driving a car forward along an unfamiliar road while concentrating on the rear-view mirror. If will not be long before something untoward occurs.

But the psychology of management is different in the pioneering days of the change from infancy to growth, when anticipation of future success drives the organisation forward. Whereas at the change from maturity to decline the dominating sentiment of management is apprehension.

In maturity managers want to re-establish growth as this indicates progress whereas slowing momentum may be thought to reflect badly on management, suggesting a lack of ability or ambition.

The equilibrium of an economic system or company at rest would seem to indicate that an optimum position has been achieved. However, this is an unstable position as all organisations are in constant motion along the lifespan and there is no known 'parking brake' that can be applied to hold all things in suspended animation.

Very few organisations return to the rapid growth phase having moved into maturity. Hence, mature companies attempt to accomplish virtual growth through high-risk strategies such as new product introduction, overseas expansion and the acquisition of competitors. Analyses have revealed that few instances of this kind of initiative are successful. In many cases an unsuccessful high-risk venture accelerates the company along the lifespan, often moving it from maturity to decline and thereby creating the turbulence that management is trying to avoid.

If a company or organisation is in maturity the strategic option most likely to benefit stakeholders would appear to have as its objective increasing the duration of the maturity phase and consistently harvesting the rewards though long-term incremental progress. Of course pressure exerted by institutional shareholders for quarterly performance data militates against this.

Many large organisations tend to consist of a sum of parts each of which may be at a different stage of its lifespan.

Few companies adopt, what appears to be, the counterintuitive strategy of breaking up the empire into smaller units, to allow each unit to pursue its own lifespan unencumbered. There are some arguments in favour of conglomerate diversification when counter cyclical businesses subsidise others. But, where this argument cannot be made, turbulent times are usually considered to be the least appropriate to embark on major strategic initiatives that throw the organisation deliberately into further and avoidable disorder. However, if the whole is unsustainable an organised restructuring is preferable to a forced sale of assets under conditions of financial distress.

If the organisation is in decline then dreams of returning to the high growth of the earlier stage are no longer credible and the objective must be to eliminate the psychology of fear and return the enterprise to stability and, probably at best, establish a period of sub-optimal maturity that is less rewarding than the earlier stage of maturity. Some damage will have been incurred, but survival with the prospect of some diminished quality of life is acceptable given the alternative of terminal collapse.

Turbulence caused by a HILPE

In much of this book I have concentrated on managing during times of general turbulence such as a recession or financial crisis, but it would be incomplete if I did not also comment about managing the effects of high impact, low probability events (HILPEs).

These are extraordinary occurrences that are the organisational equivalent of a large meteorite colliding with Earth. They happen very infrequently and consequently are rarely planned for, but their impact can be devastating.

For example, few people in government, regulation or the business arena foresaw the global financial crisis of 2008. The virtual closure of the interbank lending market was regarded as such an unlikely event that there were no plans in place to inject liquidity or rectify the sudden collapse of interbank trust.

The consequences of this low probability event have been devastating and the world economy will take many years to recover.

On a smaller scale I must address the two types of turbulence that are caused by HILPEs:

1. An organisation that encounters a HILPE the impact of which is restricted to it.

2. When a HILPE occurs during a time of general turbulence and exacerbates the problems being confronted by a single organisation.

In the first category I include such things as a food manufacturer having to recall product because of a bacteriological hazard found in the factory. This has happened with manufacturers of infant milk products in which salmonella has been discovered in their process plant. Not only must product be recalled but new product cannot be manufactured at the contaminated plant until it has been stripped down, cleaned and passed bio-inspection.

At the same time the brand is damaged to the extent that putting into the market replacement product manufactured in an uncontaminated plant may not reassure consumers and alleviate the sales decline. If an alternative brand is available to consumers few, if any, will take even a small risk with their child's health in order to follow their previous brand preference.

The turbulence resulting from this kind of event can be so catastrophic that the company may not survive. The impact comes without warning and immediately eradicates the company's market credibility by destroying the reliability of its brand. A further example of turbulence creating a loss of trust.

Legal action from retailers and consumers may further complicate matters.

Management must act very rapidly to assure retailers and consumers that either the problem never existed or that the contaminated plant has been taken completely out of production and all product on the shelves comes from an alternative clean facility.

Any hesitation or lack of conviction will magnify the problem, which will become irredeemable, sometimes within days.

The rapidity with which such a collapse occurs is why it is strongly recommended that companies vulnerable to such effects should not try to anticipate specific HILPEs, by definition this is not possible, but should prepare detailed plans for the general class that can be activated immediately.

Such preparation is not dissimilar to the logic of organising fire drills in office buildings or listening to safety presentations on aircraft or ships.

Consider the significant problem associated with the financial crisis of 2008. No-one saw it coming and there was no prepared response. Bankers and governments took months to evaluate the problem and formulate a response, by which time the original problem had magnified into a crisis of economic nuclear proportions.

The action required to manage the crisis was more extensive than would have been the case if the early implementation of a prepared plan had minimised collateral damage. For example, if central banks had a stronger mandate to regulate the interbank market by compensating rapidly for any signs of diminishing liquidity and the reluctance of banks to lend to each other. Acting as the lender of last resort does not fulfil this preventative function, as the central bank is positioned only as a safe haven when a crisis has already arisen.[10]

It doesn't take a great deal of imagination to identify some of the HILPEs to which your organisation is exposed and to plan your response. Of course it is impossible to identify them all but that is no justification for doing nothing.

The second case of encountering a HILPE while you are confronting general turbulence has a somewhat higher probability of occurring than the first case.

This is because the general turbulence creates widespread instability and the complexity of the interrelated networks which shape our social and economic system mean that not all events can be predicted and, while major disturbances arise unexpectedly, they are more likely in turbulent times when general instability is prevalent.

---

[10] As an aside I wonder why the central bank does not demand that the cash balances of all banks operating within its regulatory orbit must be deposited with it and that, if a bank wished to borrow in the interbank market, it must do so exclusively through the central bank. This method seems to obviate the potential loss of trust between banks that asphyxiated the interbank market during the second half of 2008.

For example, in a recession a major company (A) may collapse or file for bankruptcy protection from its creditors and leave a large uninsured bad debt in one of your customers (B) or suppliers (C) which destabilises them.

The consequence to you is that either your large customer (B) cannot pay you and may collapse to leave a bad debt (which insurance may cover) and a large gap in your revenue expectation (which insurance will not cover). Or your supplier (C), for which there is no readily available alternative source, might leave you with a potential production problem of significant proportions.

Either or both of these events originate at a distance from you and, because they are remote, the possibility was never factored into your plans as a potential risk but, through your interconnectedness, it manifests itself as a significant incident for which you are unprepared.

Suffice it to say that these events which arise beyond your horizon and may be low probability, but deliver a high impact, cannot be ignored as a category just because each event cannot be identified specifically.

It is frequently noted that when things are going badly you often encounter another inconvenient and unexpected negative incident that adds to the general instability (the adage *trouble always comes in threes* like all such maxims is probably based on an empirical truth).

While we may not be able to trace the causality I suggest that this pattern arises too frequently for it to be chance. Otherwise we would not have established the adage in our folk memory.

* * * *

Let me attempt to summarise the interrelationship between the organisational lifespan, the prevailing psychology of management and the optimum strategy.

Phase of Lifespan	Likely Management Psychology	Optimum Strategy	Ideal Management Psychology
Infancy	Beginning Anticipation (Becoming)	Put down supporting root system	Anticipation & developing (Becoming #1)
Growth		Maximise diffusion to exceed critical mass	
Maturity	Complacency (Being)	Extend duration of phase	Control (Being)
Decline	Fear (Reversal)	Stabilise and re-establish maturity in a structurally modified form	Confidence and Creativity (Becoming #2)
Crisis		Re-shape to ensure survival of some viable part or relieve pain of death	Determination and Ingenuity (Stabilising)

The changes in managerial psychology are crucial. In commercial enterprises the managerial elite fear being classified as ineffective as they preside over a movement from one lifespan phase to the next. The turbulence tests a manager's capabilities in the public arena and, following the growth phase, managers attempt initially, and mostly unsuccessfully, to move back to the previous phase as this is known to be comparatively comfortable ground. Especially if their reputation was established in this previous phase.

It is unlikely that those individuals who have adopted one psychological state that has led them to be successful can modify their behaviour in order to operate effectively in the succeeding phase. An individual who has become consumed by the fear of failure in the early decline phase is unlikely to change to exude confidence. Such apparent changes lack credibility both internally and externally. Similarly, a manager who exudes the now misplaced confidence of maturity during a period of general turbulence may be seen as dangerously complacent.

Up to a point an organisation tends to reflect the psychology of the person who occupies the most senior position. When a change in the psychology is necessary, this usually is most effectively accomplished by changing the individual to someone who has both experience of operating effectively in the phase into which the organisation is moving and possesses the psychology appropriate to this phase.

7

Stories

Managing through turbulent times is a story about stories. Management techniques are the tools used to control organisations but they are deployed in response to and in anticipation of events described in stories.

Stories have a powerful social function. They manipulate the mood and expectation of an audience. They can elevate the storyteller to the position of leader. They can bind together a community to pursue a common purpose and give coherent meaning to what otherwise might degenerate into chaos. At root they aim to communicate a clear vision and to work both at the rational and the emotional level in order to motivate listeners to take a given course of action with conviction and determination.

Stories told in turbulent times provide a synthesis of the turmoil which surrounds people. Initially, they may be dismissive of the negatives as the descent into turbulence begins. But, eventually, they are replaced by new stories that describe, and sometimes amplify, the threat to well-being, explain the route to salvation and the return to the stability that people crave.

Economic systems are driven by confidence and sentiment and it has been argued that the stories of impending doom contribute significantly to the turbulence that exposes the weakness of a potentially unstable system.

Accusations are levelled at the media for broadcasting speculation drawn from minimal facts. Journalists respond by claiming that they do no more than report what is or ought to be in the public arena.

The real pattern of causation is difficult to ascertain and, probably, the truth is that the media and sentiment feed on each other, such that a rumour can be disseminated and amplified until it becomes regarded as reality and attempts to deny or dispel the rumour are seen as evasion and attempts at concealment, thereby reinforcing the story.

Often stories that touch an audience's fears or hope are more powerful than the less dramatic reality. People want to believe that the turbulence will end and that normality will be restored sooner rather than later. A story which draws this conclusion will be accepted more readily than an alternative that envisions continued uncertainty and hardship without prospect of an end in the foreseeable future. We all prefer hope to despair.

A senior manager within a company who shares a nightmare scenario of impending collapse is unlikely to motivate employees to make extraordinary coordinated efforts to avoid this disastrous vision. But an individual who can find a narrative that also touches employees' hopes and describes a path along which they might be realised will motivate people to accomplish objectives they believed were beyond their grasp.

Stories were the principal tool of the great orators of history. They didn't utilise rhetoric because they were ignorant of the techniques we now call management science. They did so because it was effective. From the time of Homer, and maybe earlier, they realised that stories were the most powerful device for encouraging a group of disparate potential followers to engage in coordinated objective centred action.

Stories were also the main way in which warnings and learnings from history were remembered and passed between generations.

In later chapters on planning I advocate the use of a technique known as scenario planning. Central to this technique is the combination of subjective information with objective data to construct a story of the possible future.

The information on which managers base their decisions is incomplete and inaccurate so the deficiencies are made good by weaving the data into a story which places the data into a context and interprets it in a form that is easily remembered and communicated.

I believe that it is the quality of rhetoric and the coherent content of their stories that is one of the prime features that distinguish a leader from a manager.

But who are these individuals, the leaders, who are able to win this battle against turbulence and exert such influence over other human beings and what is it that they do?

Although we believe, almost subliminally, that we know what leadership is and that we can recognise a leader when we meet, hear or see one, this confidence is formed largely from stories about historical characters. These heroic characters may be real but their stories were composed by others, sometimes long after the event, and are probably embellished by the fictional exaggerations of the narrators. The stories developed not as objective documents and statements of record but to impress, to teach and to inspire, and it may be that what they describe is a gross distortion of the actual events on which they are based. They describe not what leaders were but what the narrators inferred that their readers would want to believe were the, often superhuman, accomplishments and virtues of individuals who, in turbulent times, emerged to achieve extraordinary things from which many benefited.

I deal with leadership more fully in chapter 8.

The stories are mythological. Intended to inspire by leaving listeners with a sense of awe and a belief that seemingly impossible tasks can be accomplished, albeit by extraordinary individuals.

These stories are the memes[11] of leadership which have infected our critical perception. For example, the exaggeration of dominant characteristics leads us towards the belief that Hitler and Stalin were entirely evil in all things and that Nelson Mandela is entirely good. Such singularity is improbable because it is not human, but this is the most memorable characterisation and it has been magnified by a convergent system that concentrates on strengthening the popular preconceptions until the predominant attribute is exaggerated to the point of caricature.

An important fraction of the uncertainty of turbulent times results from the rapidity with which the prevailing stories are discredited and new stories replace them. The next section discusses a controversial mechanism by which, it is proposed, these stories are disseminated.

---

[11] Susan Blackmore (*The Meme Machine*, 1999) defines a meme as; *"instruction(s) for behaviour(s) and communications that can be learned by imitation broadly defined."* i.e. memes can be copied using language, memory or other mechanisms and can be stored in a brain or any form of memory device.

Memes

Memes are an idea introduced by Richard Dawkins in his 1976 book *The Selfish Gene*. They are defined as units of cultural information that have certain similarities to genes. The *Oxford English Dictionary* extends this by defining a meme as, *'an element of culture that may be considered to be passed on by non-genetic means, especially imitation'*. Stanovich[12] defines a meme as, *'a brain control (or informational) state that can potentially cause fundamentally new behaviours and/or thoughts when replicated in another brain.'*

The concept of memes is important to management through turbulent times because success depends crucially on the modification of attitudes, beliefs and modes of behaviour of others.

The key point is that memes replicate. They are passed from brain to brain by word of mouth, through text, through pictures or by imitation. A good example is gossip. A piece of information that the host is seemingly compelled to transmit to as many other brains as she can. During its dissemination the original meme may interact with other memes to form a new meme that represents a distorted story that is more likely to be accepted by a recipient, thereby enhancing replication. The process of replication is analogous to viral infection of a population.

It has been hypothesised that mankind's compulsion to invent more rapid broadcast communication methods is an indirect function of our memetic complex's impulsion to greater replication through non-interpersonal means.

---

[12] *The Robot's Rebellion*; Keith Stanovich.

The question may not be how do people acquire beliefs but how do beliefs acquire people?

It is possible that, through the preservative function of literature, a meme that reaches a contemporaneous dead end may enter a phase analogous to suspended animation until it is read again, enters a new mind and a new thread begins.

This explains how the experience and learning from the previous time of economic turbulence can become 'lost' to the latest generation of managers but, in theory, may be regained.

Mankind, like many other biological entities, possesses genetically encoded instincts for subordination, followership and leadership but, unlike other biological entities, mankind is able to moderate these through the partially controllable effect of memes acting singularly or, more often, in combination with other memes as a memeplex.

When instability is significant a new person with a new and compelling narrative seems able to achieve more than an existing manager who is seen to have presided over the deterioration and was the advocate of a discredited narrative.

In turbulent times leaders are important. The times are extraordinary and people believe that, as history teaches, at times of great threat an individual emerges who can lead us to a better situation. Only rarely is this person the incumbent manager. Mostly potential followers believe that the leader will not be someone they know who is a member of the current management elite.

A new person personifies 'becoming' rather than 'reversing'.

In the political arena we can see this in the example of Winston Churchill's replacement of Neville Chamberlain in 1940, and when

Franklin D. Roosevelt replaced Herbert Hoover as US president in 1933.

We can see a new coach often motivating the players of a losing sporting team to begin to win.

We can also see this with Carlos Ghosn when he succeeded in rejuvenating the ailing Nissan in 1999/2000 and Mitt Romney's rescue of the Salt Lake City Winter Olympics in 2002.

The point is that a new individual brings a new story unencumbered by the legacy of previous narratives and, as such, is seen to personify a new phase of 'becoming'.

The ancien régime is at an end and with it the turbulence may begin to abate.

But recruiting a new person to bring a new story is never a first resort.

In each phase of the lifespan or when turbulent times are predicted the manager must recognise the need for a new story. Adhering to the existing story or attempting to re-introduce the narrative of an earlier phase rarely motivates employees.

A new story is required and managers should devote time to constructing this. The narrative should not be presented in the form of a PowerPoint presentation, which is often used to suggest deep analysis and that overly simplistic solutions have been avoided. You may use this medium in dialogue with close colleagues and in formulating detailed plans, but the meme that you want to introduce to the population in general must be simple and memorable.

The key proposition must be refined and reduced to one short paragraph and ideally compressed into a single diagram.

Employees must be able to:

1. Remember the essence of the story and be able to repeat it accurately and understand how their day to day activity relates to it.

2. Identify what they must do that is different to the pattern of work that has become habitual.

3. Appreciate how their action contributes to the rectification of the problems being experienced.

Remember also that, with some modification, this story must be the same as the narrative that you will communicate to other stakeholders.

Managing through turbulent times is not about the application of a technical fix by an astute and proficient manager but about being able to motivate a group of disheartened and demotivated people, who may be in fear of the loss of their livelihood, to act with conviction to achieve objectives they began to believe were beyond their reach. Stories are fundamental in achieving this and the memes of which they are comprised represent one of the most powerful tools available to the manager.

8

Managers or leaders?

Within the corporate arena I believe that it is possible to make a clear distinction between managers and those individuals who many people call leader. I suggest the following distinction:

Leader Type	Principal Characteristics
Type 1 The Guide	Event (change) maker Comfortable with radical change Able to influence the entire organisation Charismatic (übermensch[13]) Attracts voluntary followers Represent the whole to the parts
Type 2 The Commander	Limited to narrow, functional and incremental change Executive/guardian Operate like military commanders Represent their part to the whole
Type 3 The Icon/Model	Opinion and/or style leader Operate like religious evangelists Represent a single dimension

The Guide predominates in the political arena but is necessary in the corporate arena during the decline phase of the company's lifespan when rehabilitation is the objective.

A feature of *The Guide* is that this type of leader cannot be imposed on followers (which is not the case with *The Commander*). Followers choose to be led by this individual. I do not mean that followers should nominate leader candidates but, for the type 1 leader and follower bond to be formed and be effective, potential followers must be free to choose not to enter into the leader/follower contract. The bond between them is formed at an emotional level.

---

[13] Friedrich Nietzsche introduced this term in *Thus Spoke Zarathustra* to describe the concept of an individual who could accomplish extraordinary things.

The Commander is found most often in the military arena and is susceptible to emerging from the established elite.

If elites are allowed to nominate and impose their candidates or even to claim leadership without the consent of the majority of those who they would classify as followers then they will tend to choose a candidate from amongst their peers and superiors and never from their hierarchical subordinates.

While the commander/subordinate contract is involuntary and takes the form of a hierarchical power relationship it may, in certain cases, mature into a voluntary bond where the power is deployed fairly and responsibly.

For the most part the bond is formed on a rational basis, often with the sanction that a follower's failure to accept domination will attract some form of undesirable penalty.

The commander is what, in the corporate arena, has become known as the manager.

The Icon is most readily associated with belief systems and lifestyles and is therefore the style of leadership most readily associated with the religious arena.

The bond between the iconic leader and followers is an unspecific recipe of the emotional and rational, in that belief is a rational conclusion but in the absence of evidential support is based substantially on faith.

While it is a credible hypothesis to propose that the three leadership types are spread across the political, religious, military and corporate arenas with individuals exhibiting combinations of characteristics, it is in the corporate arena where all three styles appear to dominate at various phases of the organisational lifespan.

I suggest that this pattern tends to be as follows:

Leadership Style	Lifespan Phase	Mode
Type 3 – The Icon	Infancy and Growth	Beginning and Becoming #1
Type 2 – The Commander	Maturity	Being
Type 1 – The Guide	Decline and Rehabilitation	Becoming #2

Managers administer, maintain and enhance the operating efficiency of the organisation through organisational structure and control mechanisms, but the reactionary nature of their activity leads to inflexibility and irrelevance as the competitive landscape changes.

The kind of individual that is sought during turbulent times is the type 1 leader, The Guide.

A type 1 leader is required to reshape the organisation, reintroduce flexibility, to give it forward momentum and to reposition it. They are also required to implant and direct change to the extent that it is a 'phase transition'. Such change eschews the position that may result from a continuation of recent trends and seeks to move the organisation rapidly to a new and more conducive position from which a wider range of strategic possibilities are available.

Type 1 leaders are charismatic and persuasive but are also analytical planners. They must be achievers because the alternative to their achievement is organisational collapse.

A successful *Guide* may hold but not deploy the authority of the CEO and chairman and instead use the position as a platform to achieve compliance by projecting his or her charisma.

Followers realise that *The Guide* has the authority to command but respect him or her for not using it in a way that emphasises their subordination. Consequently, the type 1 leader avoids the creation or perpetuation of an environment in which subordinates only act in response to instructions and, instead, creates a system in which followers act in a self-motivated way moderated by their desire to demonstrate that they are of one mind with the leader and not to show that his faith in them is misplaced. It is the commonly understood story that binds them.

This regime of responsibility and recognition is not as exposed to failure through a breakdown in communication down a hierarchy.

Guides are research-oriented sceptics and do not rely on the information presented to them. They are also individuals who make the greatest use of stories and are most adept at constructing and communicating them.

People want to follow these individuals because they are perceived, through their stories, to pursue achievable goals which contribute to the enhancement of each individual's welfare.

These narratives are formulated to help followers to prepare a mental model of who they are, where they come from, the problems they face and the destination.

The stories offer followers a realistic and perhaps optimistic synthesis to replace the model of failure and pessimism that has come to predominate. In threatening situations there is an understandable receptiveness to a credible message that provides both meaning and hope to followers. The storyteller becomes the personification of the narrative.

Leaders are not messianic visionaries who seek to realise unrealistic dreams. They understand, perhaps intuitively, that their narrative is received both rationally and emotionally and that followers need to find it satisfying on both levels for them to bond with the leader and be guided to take novel and perhaps radical action.

The story that resonates with followers must also be sufficiently simple to be memorable and to be repeated with fidelity. If it is simplistic it will lack credibility so the story must compress within it unspoken wider and deeper truths that listeners are able to unpack.

What is a leader?

We've tried to define a leader since before Plato wrote *The Statesman* and still there is no consensus. Indeed, the very concept of leadership is contested with some claiming it is reification, an illusion created by the common psychological need of concerned followers to have someone who personifies their ideology and gives hope for salvation. We seem to have the rational capacity to recognise the absence of leadership demonstrated by society's persistent demand. We also know why we want to be led; because the situation to which we are exposed has moved from good to bad and is predicted to become worse unless something is done.

On the other hand, if the situation changes from bad to good we tend not to feel the same desire to be led. So we might conclude that leadership is a concept associated with giving and accepting direction in crises, and leaders are those who succeeded where more conventional types faced imminent defeat.

But we still don't agree on the full set of characteristics that differentiate a leader from the rest of us and enable us to recognise embryonic leaders.

The common position is that leaders are charismatic, probably eccentric, good communicators, who, in less challenging times, have a history of being disruptive. There may even be a clinical explanation that leaders suffer from something called narcissistic personality disorder. Their virtues are imagination, preparedness to consider the unconventional path, and an ability to navigate this route with an enthusiasm and confidence that inspires others to follow them voluntarily.

- Leaders are chameleon in that they are able and prepared to modify their behaviour to motivate each individual who interacts directly with them. They do not expect these individuals to change to align themselves with some iconic stance projected by the leader/guide.

- They motivate not through fear or coercion but by persuading others that they can achieve goals they thought beyond their capabilities.

- They are eccentric. They are unpredictable.

- They are self-sufficient and are often loners.

- They are exciting to work with, intolerant of mediocrity, impatient and frustrating in their unwillingness to conform.

- They are authoritative but non-hierarchical.

Moreover, despite attempts to teach leadership, we still perceive leaders to be in very short supply.

There comes a point in the lifespan where, without a leader, a company will probably not succeed in making transitional changes for the better. But the leader's propensity to instigate change can be detrimental if they are allowed to remain in position as the guiding authority for too long.

Leaders are dangerous individuals. The very nature of their work in instigating significant change in challenging situations means that they cannot rely on the approval of everyone and, in the course of their activity, some people will be disadvantaged or proved wrong.

There is almost always an opposing group that believe that if the status quo is maintained all will eventually be well. We can observe recent examples of this in the political arena.

Margaret Thatcher confronted the British mineworkers by arguing that their industry was uneconomical and would not be subsidised by the state. The miners preferred the status quo. Thatcher's position prevailed but she was tarnished by the concomitant social disruption.

Nelson Mandela confronted the prevailing apartheid government of South Africa who preferred the status quo to any meaningful extension of rights to the indigenous majority of citizens. Mandela lived to see the change he advocated but he is not regarded with affection by those whose interests were affected negatively.

Who are the leaders?

Many individuals claim to be leaders simply because they occupy positions of power at the top of some hierarchy. But true leaders are usually accorded the title retrospectively on the basis of exceptional achievement and not because they occupied this or that position.

There are good examples of this in the historical records of both politics and business.

In politics some of the relatively recent positive leader candidates are, Ghandi, Churchill, F.D. Roosevelt, Margaret Thatcher, Mandela, Gorbachev and as negative leaders, Hitler, Stalin, Mussolini and Pol Pot.

In business, Ken Lay of Enron and Bernard Madoff were fêted as leaders until it was discovered that their apparent success was a financial illusion. In the UK, Sir Fred Goodwin of RBS was regarded as a leader when, in August 2007, shareholders approved the GBP 50bn acquisition of Dutch bank ABN Amro. In early 2008 he declared RBS's financial position to be satisfactory but in April the bank needed to launch a GBP 12bn call for new capital to bolster its damaged balance sheet, and by the end of 2008 it needed to be rescued from imminent collapse by emergency funds from the UK government. By early 2009 he was regarded by many as a deficient manager who failed to control the business risks.

The return of Steve Jobs to Apple in 1998 is an example of the successful leader. In this case operating in an industry of persistent turbulence.

Carlos Ghosn, the Brazilian CEO of Nissan and Renault, performed what is arguably one of the most spectacular corporate turnarounds of recent times. He became CEO of Nissan in 2001 when the car manufacturer had debts of USD 20bn and a loss before interest and tax of USD 6.1bn. Within a year he converted the loss into a profit of USD 2.7bn and Nissan developed to return the best operating margins in its sector.

There are other examples; Mitt Romney's rescue of the 2002 Salt Lake City Winter Olympics, Stuart Rose at Marks & Spencer.

What these stories reveal is that sometimes the apparent initial success of those who are called leaders conceals catastrophic failure but also that you do not need to resort to bankruptcy law to rescue a troubled business in turbulent times if you have the right leadership.

Leadership is not superior management, it is a different skill. Abraham Zaleznik argued this in his classic, 1977 article in *Harvard Business Review*. He claimed, controversially, that managers address problems by selecting actions from an established catalogue of processes whereas leaders are successful because they tend to formulate original solutions to problems managers find intractable.

I think Zaleznik was right and I would add, contextually, that we seek leadership mostly when conditions deteriorate from being stable or comfortable to turbulent and threatening. This may be because corporate management changes focus from manoeuvring for competitive positioning to managing for stability.

When an economic storm is imminent the manager's methodical framework, consisting in the conventional techniques of planning and control, becomes unreliable. The managerial toolbox and psychology are not equipped to deal effectively with turbulence and cannot handle crises, and they cannot implement systematic programmes to develop a business when the medium term is hidden behind a cloud of uncertainty.

So is it the result of poor direction by the Board or just bad luck that, in turbulent times, companies collapse and others are so badly damaged that they continue as the disabled corporate victims for years to come?

Luck plays its part in every business but bad *direction* is not the only contributory factor to unnecessary corporate collapse; the wrong *kind* of guiding mind is just as significant. Too few directors and shareholders appreciate the distinction between leadership and management and fewer still understand when a managerial guiding mind should be replaced by a leader.

Managers cannot become leaders on demand

When an organisation encounters a crisis its managers often try but usually are unable to transform themselves into leaders with any credibility. They continue to employ their managerial toolkit but adopt the demeanour of iconic leaders (Churchillian, Napoleonic and the fictional US President in *The West Wing* are favourite stereotypes) but onlookers are usually unconvinced. The manager's new style is what it is; an ersatz leader beneath which the psychology of the manager persists.

Managerial politicians often refer to themselves as leaders and change the tone of their rhetoric in response to the emergence of crisis. Prime Minister Gordon Brown arguably provides a good example of a well regarded manager struggling to transform himself into a leader. He was regarded as a technically proficient Chancellor who believed the skills that made him successful in that job equipped him to become PM. In stability he might have succeeded, but in the midst of a crisis the public looks for someone whom they can regard as a leader, an individual who has the charisma to reassure them that their worst fears can be overcome. Prior to the financial crisis Brown could only attempt to imitate the way he perceived true leaders behaved, but the artificiality of this prosthetic personality was utterly unconvincing and left Mr Brown with the worst rating for public confidence since Neville Chamberlain confronted his crisis in 1940. Of course the financial crisis presented him with turbulence in the area in which his reputation was highest and thus provided the ideal situation in which he had a credible claim to competency.

Others see leadership as benign dictatorship or even a form of authoritarianism. A movement in this direction is the natural tendency of those in power when any crisis emerges, however someone with authority but without the voluntary approval of followers is not a leader. Leaders motivate followers to achieve the unexpected not through coercion but through inspiration.

In business and politics the individuals who can accomplish this are rarely found amongst the incumbent elite management team and there are compelling arguments that the changes he or she must personify can only be instigated effectively by an unconnected outsider.

Beware hubris

Nor is the successful leader the sovereign who, as a reward for providing salvation, is awarded the crown in perpetuity. It is a negative feature of their narcissism and egoism that so many have been seduced in this way.

Carlos Ghosn was given the crown at Nissan and also simultaneously at Renault. He has been unable to sustain Nissan's performance or do the same thing for Renault, and by 2007 his star was tarnished by falling earnings.

The recent dispute at Marks & Spencer about the extension of Sir Stuart Rose's tenure and his elevation to executive chairman is suggestive of this. In the political arena the attempt by Margaret Thatcher to remain in office in 1990 when her support had evaporated and Churchill's campaign to hold onto power in 1945 are further examples.

Leaders are recruited to achieve specific objectives, typically to overcome an imminent threat and return the organisation to stability in a form that enables it to prosper. Once this task has been accomplished and the turbulence has subsided the leader must step down and the task of rebuilding and consolidation passed to the supervision of someone with the organisational and administrative skills of the manager.

When to discard a leader

I suggest that the dominant style of an organisation's guiding mind must change when there is a material deterioration in its performance or prospects. If a period of extended stability has resulted in managerialism becoming embedded then the organisation should change to leadership orientation and vice versa.

The classic example of this transition from manager to leader followed by a hubristic attempt to retain power and the return to managerial orientation is that of Neville Chamberlain's replacement in 1940 by Winston Churchill, followed by his replacement at the height of his success by Clement Atlee.

Chamberlain and Atlee were accomplished managerial politicians possessing administrative skills that were the antithesis of Churchill's attributes. In the critical situation of 1939, Prime Minister Chamberlain's attempt to tackle the turbulence by the managerial technique that we recognise as logical incrementalism failed totally and war with Germany followed. With the threat of invasion imminent in 1940, Churchill, the renegade, eccentric, inspiring, communicatively gifted loose cannon replaced Chamberlain as Prime Minister and his success and the adoration it brought are well documented.

By 1945 his objective of winning the war had been achieved but he wanted to retain power. The electorate recognised that the emerging situation presented no military threat and was no longer apposite to Churchill's skills but required someone with the comparatively mundane organisational abilities of Atlee. Atlee became PM in Churchill's place and the cycle of manager to leader to different manager over the six-year duration of the crisis that was World War II was complete.

You can follow the same path with Margaret Thatcher's replacement of James Callaghan's premiership in 1979 following the winter of discontent and her own enforced replacement by the managerially inclined John Major.

Political analogies are important to business leadership for two reasons. Firstly the concepts of business management copy principles honed in the military and political arenas. Secondly, they provide a more objective public record of the conduct of individuals from which executives draw their role models. Although, paradoxically, these stories also contain the lesson that managerial incumbents cannot acquire or successfully imitate the characteristics of a leader.

While there are few people who have the attributes and psychology to be successful where others have failed, they are not superheroes capable of unbelievable achievements in all situations. They are appropriate only to the moment and for them to hold power in calmer times is, I believe, counterproductive.

What happened to some of the great leaders of history who survived the turbulence over which they presided?

Themistocles	Ostracised
Caesar	Assassinated
Bonaparte	Imprisoned
Churchill	Fired
Ghandi	Assassinated
Mandela	Imprisoned
Thatcher	Fired

Leadership is a dangerous business.

The removal of the leader who has either become dangerous, hubristic, ineffective or offensive to the sensibilities of some opposing group is akin to sacrifice in a religious context. There is a residual belief that by conferring upon on a prominent scapegoat, the evil that attends and then driving the individual out of public life the 'evil' will be removed, atonement achieved and a fresh start made. Leaders are associated with a time of danger and discord that people wish to consign to history with alacrity.

We can return to the example of Lehman and ask whether the CEO Dick Fuld who led the bank from a difficult period to become a dominant Wall Street institution had become hubristic and whether his removal at an early stage would have averted the collapse of the bank. In retrospect the answer must be yes because he dismissed warnings of potential instability by continuing to employ a successful business model beyond its limit. Significant retrenchment was inevitable but collapse was avoidable.

However, modern transitional events are rarely the personal action of a single powerful individual but arise when the organisation becomes seriously maladapted to externally induced distortions to its operating landscape. Removing the individual thought to be the problem does not remove the transitional event cause. Hence the removal of a manager who has presided over the movement from maturity to decline and replacement by another manager who is similarly equipped to manage stability is unlikely to reverse the trend of decline.

Leaders must appreciate that followers can tolerate only a limited amount of change that is directly proportional to the actual or potential loss they might incur from inaction. This is a function of the followers' capacity to endure stress. A long period of stability, such as that experienced during maturity, reduces followers' capacity to endure the stress of a sudden transitional event such as a surprise attack or a predatory takeover attempt.

But if they fear the consequences of inaction they will endure the stress of more far-reaching changes than if they are indifferent to the likely post event situation. For example, an order to evacuate a city will be regarded differently if the weather forecast is for a gale than would be the case if it was a category five hurricane.

The skills of the manager and the abilities of the leader and their attendant behaviour patterns are unlikely to be possessed by the same person as they are, to a large degree, mutually exclusive and the associated psychologies are quite different.

Some leadership theorists advocate a continuum between managers and leaders which leads to the conclusion that there is a group of individuals who cannot be assigned wholly to either category.

I find this a difficult concept to accept as the psychology of the manager (the bureaucrat or autocrat) is so different from that of the leader that it is unlikely that there are many hybrids. Although leaders will once have been managers I cannot conceive of leaders metamorphosing into managers.

I cannot envisage Clement Atlee becoming Winston Churchill or vice versa, or FDR adopting, at will, the personality of Harry Truman.

Although leaders may once have been mangers I do not want to imply that leadership is superior to management. My thesis is that it is a different skill set.

Therefore, we must conclude that the people most likely to succeed as leaders are not those most likely to succeed as managers, and vice versa.

Having reached this idealistic conclusion it is necessary to return to pragmatism. In turbulent times not all organisations can make the change from managerialism to leadership even if the charismatic leaders were readily available. Managers must deal with the challenges.

The final chapters deal in detail with how this can be accomplished.

9

Seven principles of crisis management

Crises occur when the impact of turbulence brings the organisation to the point of collapse, where little time is available for analysis and contemplation and preventative or protective action is required urgently.

Crisis management is a term popularised by Robert McNamara when he was US Secretary of Defence during the Cuban Missile Crisis in 1962, but the process it describes can be recognised throughout recorded history.

In fact, some historians have suggested that the unfolding of history is little more than the record of how society has managed its crises.

Given mankind's long experience of crises we might be forgiven for believing that we have developed some tried and tested procedures for resolving them. Certainly interstate diplomacy trades on this belief, but we continue to encounter irreconcilable positions and wars. Business schools give courses on risk assessment and controlling turbulent situations but companies still collapse into bankruptcy.

Categorising a situation as a crisis owes much to the mental orientation of those directly involved. The focus of a crisis is the avoidance of undesirable consequences that will arise if the current trend continues and, as such, strategic goals that may have driven actions in less turbulent times must be set aside.

The objective of crisis management is not to rescue and reinvigorate the preceding strategy, it is to stabilise the organisation, assess the damage and determine what action is feasible with the resources remaining.

In extremis the course in which it is directed does not matter nor does where the organisation emerges from the crisis. What matters is that the organisation survives, is viable and has sufficient resources to enable a new strategy to be formulated when the form in which it will emerge is clear.

While there is no totally reliable road map describing the path from problem through crisis to resolution there are some guidelines which are set out below and that have served me well. The key is the quality of the content that fills each of the 7 principles.

1. Obtain multiple opinions in the decision-making process

2. Retain close control over the implementation of policy

3. Reduce time pressure

4. Limit objectives

5. Maintain flexible options

6. Understand the nature and potential behaviour of the adversary

7. Maintain communication

I deal below with each principle in more detail.

1. Obtain multiple opinions in the decision-making process

Thinking alone is a dangerous process that can easily lead to depression or delusion, but often managers confronted by turbulent times feel that sharing their anxiety with colleagues and especially outsiders is to reify their concern, making inevitable that which, for the moment, seems only possible.

Turbulent times induce stress and this tends to increase an individual's inflexibility. Their tolerance of ambiguity also diminishes as they seek to simplify the perceived complexity of the situation in order to configure it in readily understood terms for which there is an established methodology in the managerial toolkit which may slow the pace of change to a more comfortable rate.

A dominant view may come to prevail that, in turn, is defended and all information is subsequently filtered through this conclusion to be rejected if it is contradictory. This means that important data may be disregarded as it reinforces a correct but unacceptable perception of complexity and instability.

Often a group dynamic is also at work. Privately, managers may have similar concerns to a greater or lesser extent but these are not voiced in meetings because doing so is perceived to be a kind of corporate heresy. No-one wants to be the one who says *the Emperor is naked*!

It is this discord that is represented on the vertical axis of the T-matrix.

Eventually this position becomes unsustainable and, to the relief of some and the apprehension of others, the elephant in the room has to be recognised and discussed otherwise the consequence is chaos.

This is when denial often moves to concealment. The issues are recognised but the discussion is confined to a small group who are sworn to secrecy because people tend to believe that if their concerns were to be widely disseminated the problem would be magnified. The intention is to formulate a solution to resolve the difficulties or avoid further deterioration before any suspicion of instability enters the wider arena.

When input is limited to a few insiders the problem is that bias and myopia becomes likely, especially if this is the same group that denied the existence of a problem. At its worst the result can be the development of factionalism.

Managing through turbulent times requires perspective. You cannot see through the storm and no longer have confidence in your navigational equipment so how are you able to steer the ship towards safety?

The ideal is for someone or something located outside the closed system of your vessel to introduce new data or an alternative interpretation of the situation that compensates for your information deficiency and obviates your need to rely exclusively on unsubstantiated or uninformed guesses.

Satellite navigation performs exactly this function, except in the corporate world a similar device is not part of the manager's toolkit.

So the methodology is to obtain opinions and ideas from a wide spectrum of people ideally offering opposing points of view. Don't disregard or down-weight opinions that disagree with your own or are uncomfortable. Sometimes your discomfort is your intuition telling you that there is a truth inherent in what is being said that you have suppressed.

In this wide spectrum include external people who are experienced in crisis management and who are dispassionate and, unlike insiders, have no emotional inhibitions to prevent them from proposing solutions that may damage projects, power base, relationships or reputations.

Only when you have consulted widely and have recognised your own bias and inhibition can you evaluate the options, but then action must be decisive.

As a senior manager the decision about which direction to take may be yours alone. Consensus is fine when you have it but, in turbulent times, seeking it must not delay action. This is not licence for autocracy but the simple recognition that the urgency of the situation means that there is always a point at which a course must be chosen.

You are embarking on a journey but the only information you have is your starting point (turbulence) and a general destination (stability). You have no map and no time to plan the most direct route. Turbulent times mean that you must move rapidly to avoid the undesirable consequences of remaining in your starting location.

Nor is this a one-off exercise. You must continue to solicit impartial opinions for as long as the turbulence persists and from time to time add or substitute a new voice.

They only way in which you can find your route is to ask people who you meet along the way and who might be better informed and to keep asking as you travel.

2. Retain close control over the implementation of policy

The problem is that, at or close to the onset of turbulence, it is often difficult to establish a prognosis. Few can state with compelling authority that some minor disturbance is the initial symptom of crisis.

As we have discussed it is not unusual at an early stage to recognise that conditions are changing but to deny that this will cause a significant detrimental impact to your organisation. Those who predict a severe impact are, at an early stage, often marginalised as exaggerators and pessimists. The descent into crisis is always decorated with false optimism.

But once delusion has been set aside and reality prevails there can be no higher priority than overcoming an event that threatens your survival.

This must be emphasised by the activity being championed and closely controlled by the most senior executive. All other programmes and initiatives must be subordinated for the duration.

Technical competency is necessary to understand the issues, the implications and to formulate a response but this is insufficient. Senior managers must not remain remote technocrats. Stakeholders require direct reassurance that management is on top of the challenges and they gain some element of the comfort they seek from the manager's personality. In short, stakeholders draw conclusions from actions, statements, personality and body language to determine whether they feel confident that this individual's characteristics accord with what they think is required for the situation. Previous achievements tend not to be an asset on which the manager can rely to gain latitude and tolerance of underachievement.

Consequently, one of the greatest tests that a manager faces may be how he or she can become more charismatic and deciding whether even trying to be so is so alien to their personality that the performance would lack credibility. It would be counterproductive if, in trying to exude hope, determination and unite stakeholders to confront a common challenge, you appeared insincere and foolish.

You may regard the above as obvious but, based on their actions, many senior managers believe that the management of a crisis, whether it is unique to their company or the impact of a general malaise, should be treated like a project with a dedicated team who operate independently of the established structure which is encouraged to function normally.

I struggle to understand how this can be considered a rational response. My best guess is that it is rooted in a belief that:

- Giving management of the event to a dedicated team relieves line management of the stress and distraction of having to confront the issues.

  I suspect this can never work well in reality as people will worry more if they are unable to acquire good first-hand information about the progress of the organisation's response.

  The event probably impacts the entire organisation but for the response to be confined to a project group implies falsely that there is a technical solution which does not require wider involvement or action.

- It signals that senior management is applying a concentrated resource to the problem rather than asking a wider group to take on an additional task.

- It suggests a controlled response and, because it is confined, that the organisation has something more held in reserve.

  For managers the demonstration of control in the face of actual or potential instability is psychologically important because it brings the problem within their comfort zone, whereas instability and unpredictable complexity are anathema.

- It enables those senior managers who feel themselves unable to act to pass the problem on to others who may succeed, in which case senior managers can claim credit for directing them, or, if they fail, can carry the blame.

However, I suggest that all the above motives are a weak response by management who must either personify the response or move aside to allow someone who will head the organisation until the crisis has passed.

Culturally this latter course may present additional problems. In the corporate arena we still recruit managers on the basis that they have the professional ability to handle all situations that they may encounter and that they will remain in position until either they decide to move on to something better or until they become a liability and have to be removed from office.

In the modern organisation this is unrealistic and the shortening tenure of CEOs to an average of around 3-4 years, which is shorter than a complete business cycle, indicates that this 'manager for all seasons' notion is flawed.

If stakeholders do not feel that the most senior manager has either the experience or capability to take command of the business and manage it through turbulent times they should take action at the onset to replace him or her with someone who does, even though this may be a temporary appointment for the duration.

The management of instability is not a normal activity and those being managed understand this. A manager who fails to recognise this or attempts to disguise their own fear and stress by hiding from general view will not motivate other members of the organisation to take extraordinary action in a common cause, but will succeed only in magnifying dependent people's concern for their own well-being.

Employees are not stupid. They understand that conditions have changed and know when matters are serious. Like all stakeholders they want to see action but also it is important that they play an active role, make a contribution, feel that some fraction of the solution lies in their hands.

You must be at the centre to monitor and communicate progress towards specified objectives in an obsessive if not messianic way. You must not let the organisation come to regard the action of responding to turbulence as normality. Emphasise continually that these are special times that require extraordinary actions and that if the objectives are achieved then the instability will pass or be avoided and some version of the stability experienced in the phase of prosperity will return.

The story of the turbulent times can be presented as a journey to a new promised land of stability.

As we discussed earlier these are the moments when people crave leadership, which for some managers is hard to offer. If there has been a prolonged period of stability then most organisations have a tendency to become dominated by procedure and protocols that impose discipline and control, and managers spend the majority of their time modifying and implementing this process to minimise the risk inherent in delivering incremental growth in returns.

But turbulent times are different. They are characterised by a rapid acceleration of change usually well beyond the capacity of these established protocols to moderate the deterioration. So it becomes difficult for incumbent managers to almost instantly alter their modus operandi and stop being the enforcer of procedural compliance and adopt the role of leader.

I contend that it is not easy for a good manager of an organisation in stable times to change the dominant story and to become the leader of the same organisation in a period of turbulence. In the same way that turbulent times expose the organisation's structural and financial weaknesses, they expose managerial weaknesses and the psychological unsuitability of individuals.

But we must be pragmatic. Not all organisations can change their senior management and there is not a population of leaders standing on the sidelines waiting to be called into action. Hence the oft-heard lament of *where are today's leaders?*

Do not pretend that you have the answers. Remember that even Churchill, on becoming UK Prime Minister in the dark, crisis-ridden days of 1940, did not say that he possessed a miraculous solution. His speech of 13 May 1940 stated that:

> *"I have nothing to offer but blood, toil, tears, and sweat. We have before us an ordeal of the most grievous kind. We have before us many, many months of struggle and suffering."*

Admit that these are unusual events and that your toolkit may be deficient. Emphasise the common cause. Do not be afraid to supplement your capabilities at an early stage with outsiders; to do so is not a sign of weakness but of strength. But above all indicate that resolving the difficulties that the organisation confronts is the consuming issue on your agenda and that you will do whatever it takes to steer the organisation to stability.

3. Reduce time pressure

Identify the things that create and consume time. Focus on the former, eliminate the latter.

There is a natural wish to escape the turbulence or resolve a crisis as quickly as possible. Intuitively we all believe that the longer instability persists the greater will be the damage it inflicts as everything has a tolerance limit.

Once the time of denial has passed there is a tendency to pick up the pace and want to receive information as quickly as possible so that decisions can be made without further delay. The faster we take action the sooner the benefits will arise and vulnerability to the instability will decline is the maxim that drives this change of managerial pace.

Also, the time pressure inherent in the accelerated change of turbulent times can be compounded by the self-imposed pressure created by regarding too many things as equally urgent.

I do not want to minimise the challenges or the urgency with which you will need to address some problems but increased time pressure is a key cause of stress, which leads to poor decision-making. Complacency is equally dangerous. But decisions taken under time pressure are often ill-considered and usually incorrect. It doesn't necessarily follow that good decisions result from more time being available as this time may be squandered by hoping that the original strategy will come good. But on balance, gaining more time is preferable to finding that you have less.

In turbulent times conventional responses become unreliable and the counterintuitive becomes desirable. If the organisation can be regarded as a car then it is not necessary for the whole vehicle to move at the same speed. The organisation needs to change its shape but if it moves in a synchronised way no change will occur. Visualise making the vehicle more streamlined and better able to cut through the turbulence with minimal resistance. As your mental animation distorts the car you see some parts changing faster than others. That is the model your company needs to follow.

How can you reduce time pressure?

The transformation that arises in turbulent times progresses at double or treble the rate of change experienced in the preceding period of comparative stability and includes sudden dramatic transitions. Check out a graph of movements in the principal stock markets to confirm how the rate of change varies.

Do not become infected by the general climate of hyperactivity and attempt to operate faster in all things. To try and match the speed of events by reacting instantly to any change can be compelling as it suggests you are in control, but it is illogical and at some point this activity is best described as panic.

Human beings do have the capacity to respond to threatening situations by taking faster decisions. In the main these are the fight or flight reflexes we have developed to increase our chances of survival in the face of danger. But these are instinctive reactions to clear and present danger and not considered responses to complex issues.

It is not possible to double or treble at will the speed of your analysis and formulation of action and, at the same time, preserve a high quality of decision-making. Consequently, you must list the issues you intend to study and process and then reduce the number to the most urgent and important that your organisation has the capacity to process effectively.

So your first task as a senior manager facing a crisis or high level of turbulence is to determine what this level of organisational processing capacity is.

There is no hard and fast rule to determine this. It depends on the scale of your organisation, the complexity of the key issues, the number and the quality of the people you employ. It is a judgement issue and one that you may miscalculate initially and need to adjust quickly. It is your ability to make such judgement calls under pressure that defines you as a senior manager.

The second task is to select the issues to be addressed as discussed in rule 4 below.

Bear in mind that you can create additional time for urgent events by slowing or terminating other activities. Inevitably this means that some significant issues and projects may have their financial and human resources withdrawn.

Other things that you need to explore are:

- Resist customers or suppliers trying to pass their time pressure to you. For example, by customers requiring 'just in time' deliveries to minimise inventories, or by lenders wanting information to measure covenant compliance every month instead of every quarter.

- If creditors are pressing or you have breached, are about to breach, loan covenants or are in default of loan agreements then you should attempt to negotiate a standstill agreement by which your lenders agree not to take further action for a specified period during which you can pursue refinancing, new capital and restructuring plans in the certain knowledge that your lenders and other creditors are not going to intervene by foreclosing.

In negotiating these agreements be explicit and clear that your objective is to create a bubble of stability in which you are able to concentrate on remedial management and that it is for the benefit of all stakeholders.

The example of Premier Foods Plc given earlier illustrates the point.

Spend time planning what you and your team are going to work on over the next few weeks, thereby reducing the propensity to act spontaneously to extinguish the fire at your feet.

Appoint someone to be custodian of the administration of the programme (in large organisations this may be a new full-time job) who ensures everyone is complying with the programme by identifying their difficulties before the delivery deadline and helping to overcome them by redeploying resources etc.

If the progression of problems has reached the stage of confrontation (see page 86) following a period of denial, concealment and failed containment then the incumbent senior manager may not possess sufficient residual credibility to be given more time.

Given that the incumbent manager has advocated the preceding phase of denial and concealment, independent directors must consider whether this individual has the credibility to secure a bubble of stability and whether he or she has the attributes necessary to make the best use of the pause.

Changing the CEO may be the price that must be paid to buy the bubble of short-term stability that the organisation needs.

Change may be necessary but takes time and those newly in charge are usually given a period of time that is not available to their predecessor.

The above discussion majors on the management of time pressure from the viewpoint of someone on whom the pressure is applied. But you should also consider how your actions impose time pressure on those whose cooperation you wish to secure. It is easy to conclude that you are taking the most effective action by exerting pressure on those who, by delaying their decisions and actions, are creating problems for you, but consider whether depriving them of time by imposing threats linked to deadlines is likely to elicit from them the rational response that you desire.

Acquiring time by creating additional instability amongst associated and dependent organisations, so called collateral damage, can be counterproductive. You must be careful to ensure that the benefits of progress in one area are not negated by regression in another.

Always consider carefully the effect your action will have outside of your organisation and how this might feed back to create or magnify your problems.

Reducing time pressure is not an exercise conducted at an early stage and then allowed to run its course. It is something that you must attend to frequently in response to emergent pressures and the development of new opportunities to acquire additional time.

4. Limit objectives

Objectives should be limited in number and ordered by importance. Not over-generalised or oversimplified.

In any organisation there are probably a dozen things that people believe require urgent attention but in turbulent times there exist the resources to manage fewer than five of them effectively.

Moreover, experience suggests that only three or four things are truly crucial. Get these wrong and the other things don't matter. Get them right and most of the others may seem less daunting.

You must avoid the tendency to respond to the acceleration of general change that is a key feature of turbulence by dispersing resources in an attempt to manage all issues. Instead, you must order the pressing issues by a combination of:

(i)   their impact on stability,

(ii) those which if postponed will buy time to decelerate the slide to instability and

(iii) which singularly and in combination offer the most significant medium term benefit, and

(iv) those that are capable of achievement with the limited resources you have available.

The organisation must focus its resources on overcoming the most threatening issue and the first objective is always to create stability to ensure that the pace of decline doesn't accelerate out of control.

a.   Stability provides time and ensures that there is a consistent shape to the problem you are confronting.

b.   Creation of stability will not resolve the underlying issues but facilitate the rational formulation of clear programmes.

c. Once stability has been achieved set limited objectives for the next phase (6 to 12 months). In formulating these objectives remember that your horizon of expectation is near, which means stability is fragile and collapses if no progress is made during the short term.

d. Remember also that not all problems can be resolved in a manner that preserves the independence or shape of the subject entity. In a war territory is lost, patients lose limbs and some die, companies close operations and, in extremis, file for bankruptcy.

Trying to achieve or preserve too much will probably result in failure to achieve or preserve anything.

5. Maintain flexible options

Unshakeable commitment to a single course of action may demonstrate conviction but can be fatal.

You may feel that an overt demonstration of conviction is what is required to give stakeholders the impression that you have confidence in the plan you are presenting. You may also believe that anything less will be counterproductive as your audience is looking for a demonstration of confident determination in order to allay their fear of the risks to their interests.

But this commits you to a single plan which you advocate will resolve the problems both being experienced and predicted. If it doesn't work as advertised you have a reputational and credibility problem but the organisation cannot revert to the original position in order to adopt an alternative course.

However such certainty is inconsistent with the definition of turbulence as a state of unpredictability.

Do not succumb to the notion that you must formulate a plan and adhere to it irrespective of early signals that it may be misconceived. Remember that turbulence is accelerated change but not necessarily in a predictable direction and the conditions you anticipated when constructing the plan may not arise in the form or timescale you expected.

So I suggest four cardinal principals should guide your planning:

1. Ensure the organisation is able to change direction quickly; build in greater flexibility not less.

2. Do not pursue policies that close off access to all other options.

3. Always prepare a second plan to which you will move if the

preferred option proves inadequate and identify the specific information that will trigger the move from plan A to plan B. Plan B should be fully developed and plan C should be understood in outline.

4. Make sure plan B is funded with plan A and do not hesitate to abandon a preferred, but failing, option and move to a credible alternative.

Ensure that you include comments about increasing flexibility in the story you tell. Use metaphors such as 'any port in a storm' to emphasise that while you will navigate towards destination A, if conditions change you will divert to location B.

6. Understand the nature and potential behaviour of the adversary

Many managers conceive of the problems they face as confined to their organisation and that dependant parties are either 'on side' in helping to find a solution or are neutral. They cannot understand why any connected party would want the organisation to collapse. This is a little naïve.

Make no mistake, in every crisis there is an adversary, a party that is pursuing their own interest and will do so at the expense of yours. In the corporate arena this is often a lender represented by a bank or bondholder who has rights that may be enforced in a default situation.

A crisis is unmanageable when your adversary sees no advantage in working with you to find a mutually acceptable outcome. In many cases mutuality is superseded by the determination to secure an entirely self-centred agenda.

It is crucial to manage this relationship but too simplistic to believe that the adversary's potential loss will discourage them from exercising their rights. Your first loss is your smallest is an important banking maxim which means if the lender has no confidence that your plan will give them more than they believe they currently have, they will withdraw support.

The key is to know what they believe they currently have. If you ask they won't tell. To do so may weaken their negotiating leverage that is born of your ignorance and fear that you may not satisfy them. You must take steps to work this out for yourself.

7. Maintain communication

A crisis switches a spotlight on management. Little can be undertaken covertly so the communication of actions, initiatives and progress must be managed carefully.

If you Google 'crisis management' you will find that most pages[14] are devoted to some form of public relations activity intended to mitigate reputational damage to brand names or the public confidence in organisations when they encounter a unique problem during stable times.[15] Or when government has to manage disaster recovery. These are important areas but are not those I wish to discuss.

I want to focus on the more thinly documented area of communication and signalling in the context of specific organisations encountering problems that arise in generally turbulent times.

Poor management of communications in these situations can have a detrimental influence on the effectiveness of management programmes. Remember, the void of silence is always filled by speculation. You have no control over speculation so you need to manage the opinions of your audience. They will evaluate your actions under the new spotlight of attention in order to ascertain clues about your confidence, conviction and stature, which then will combine with the substance of the programme you advocate to determine the risk they perceive and the trust they give.

In order to bind followers to them leaders depend crucially on the way they are perceived, which explains why the acknowledged leaders throughout the historical record have tended to be exceptionally proficient communicators.

[14] 2,600,000 hits in January 2009.

[15] For example, when a malfunctioning of the Union Carbide plant at Bhopal caused widespread chemical harm to the surrounding population or what was required to overcome the BSE crisis in British beef.

In the corporate arena there are four key audiences:

1. External stakeholders

2. Suppliers

3. Customers

4. Employees

Each audience requires a nuanced version of the same message. If you are a medium to large company your difficulties will attract the interest of journalists who will have their own agenda or will simply be constrained by space and time and will therefore select the most dramatic interpretation. You must not rely on broadcast media to control the flow of information people receive but neither can you suppress the media interest.

If you are not comfortable with dealing with the media then employ professionals to act as your spokesperson, decline interviews but issue written statements, and ensure that others in your organisation are not 'briefing' externally.

External stakeholders

This category is populated predominantly by those who fear that they are likely to lose significant sums that previously they believed carried a much lower risk than has proved to be the case.

In turbulent times your organisation will not be alone in presenting an elevated risk profile to lenders, shareholders and bondholders and so control over the messages these groups use to formulate their perceptions is important in creating an atmosphere that is conducive to maintaining a positive dialogue.

Communication is comprised of three media:

1. Interpersonal dialogue

2. Written reports

3. General media comment

You have the greatest control over the documentation you prepare and circulate but communication is rarely confined to this medium.

Interpersonal dialogue should be instigated by carefully selected individuals who are thoroughly briefed to stay 'on message'. You cannot manage the interpersonal dialogue that takes place between employees but the substance of this conversation often leaks into the public domain so the input information is crucial to this. This is where you need to manage the memes.

Similarly, contact with the press and broadcast media should be channelled through a spokesperson either within the organisation or from your public relations consultancy.

(i) Shareholders

Shareholders may be able to cut their potential losses by selling into the market and your communication will influence their sentiment of whether to hold or sell. In a private company shareholders do not have a liquid market in which to sell or buy and may therefore present a greater challenge, especially if they are unsympathetic to the turbulence having arisen generally and regard the potential instability that threatens their wealth to be a symptom of managerial deficiency. A significant sub-group is the private equity funds that have been especially active in acquiring large businesses.

These groups recognise that they sit at the bottom of the list upon liquidation and if the organisation collapses it is likely that their investment will be worthless. Therefore, they seek hope and reassurance. Reassurance that bankruptcy is unlikely and hope that performance will improve.

They will appreciate that lenders and bondholders occupy positions of greater power in that they may have agreements that enable them to use events of default to call for immediate repayment unless shareholders introduce new funds to reduce the organisation's debts. Invest more or lose all that you currently have invested is a brutal proposition that no shareholder wants to face.

So shareholders are usually seeking reassurance from management that there is no short-term prospect of lenders and bondholders pushing the company towards bankruptcy.

(ii) Lenders and bondholders

Lenders and bondholders are concerned about changes to the risk of their loans not being serviced, and the possibility that, in a forced liquidation, they would not recover the principal.

The legal agreements that specify the rights and obligations associated with these loans will set out the procedures which apply in default or when management anticipates default. Usually these agreements stand alone but in the event of financial distress a default in the terms of one agreement can in itself be an event of default in others, leading to a cascade of breached agreements and the exacerbation of a problem into a financial crisis.

You must understand these terms and conditions in detail to be able to appreciate the communication and signals that counterparties want to hear that do not trigger specific action that you don't want and they may be unable to avoid.

Of course, financial tests such as asset to loan ratios are matters of fact and you cannot spin the data to mean something different. What you can do is to conduct the tests yourself on a more frequent basis and map the trend so that you can anticipate what the position is likely to be on the actual test date. You then have some advance warning of the information lenders and bondholders may receive and time to compose a narrative to accompany the bad news with detailed plans of the action you have taken or intend to take to rectify any problem, the effect you expect the action to have and when you predict the financial test will return to a compliant measure.

You must be sensitive to making too big an issue about deteriorating measures as you do not want lenders to infer that you believe that the deteriorating trend will lead inevitably to a default position. Anticipatory default and clauses which call for the notification of material adverse changes to the condition of the business are tectonic in their significance and are dependent entirely on the information you provide. Moreover, the information is, by definition, a combination of quantitative and subjective data. These things *might* happen and *might* have a detrimental effect. The perceived likelihood of this possibility becoming fact depends on the way you present the information. Remember that stakeholders expect you to be more optimistic than realistic and dilute your narrative accordingly.

If you do not believe that you have the experience or the capability to walk in this minefield then you must employ specialist external assistance. In Europe most major accounting firms have specialist staff who understand these agreements and are used to working with lenders and bondholders. In the US the expertise tends to be in law practices. In Asia the location of expertise varies by jurisdiction.

These services are expensive and tend to be used where the sums involved are large. Moreover, these advisers will not stand between you and the lenders. You will still need to explain the action you intend to take but the validation of your expectations by these professional advisers will add credibility.

If you cannot afford this level of professional assistance you should still attempt to follow the same process.

From the data you have about the financial position and prospects of your business list the conclusions you would draw if you were the lender. If you feel insufficiently objective ask someone, an independent director, your auditor or in extremis a relative or very good friend to role-play the part of the lender for you.

From the feedback you can ascertain the key messages you need to address.

Remember that in this type of communication it is not a matter of what you want to say but of what you want the reader/ listener to elicit. Also remember that your immediate contact will probably not be the only or main decision taker and will need to present your status report to others. Therefore, the key proposition has ideally to be simple, powerful and memorable.

Always present your case in writing and never rely on an oral presentation being sufficient. In oral presentations people take out only some of the information and are influenced by your body language, their time constraints and attention span.

Having secured the continued support of lenders and bondholders you should plan the future communication by producing a programme that will keep them fully apprised of developments. Try to avoid the situation in which people feel the need to call you for an update. Do not confine this to only giving good news as, in turbulent times, most people realise that the situation's unpredictability means that unexpected reverses may arise.

Do not commence a second phase of denial, concealment, etc.

Of course, acceptance of a problem followed by unalloyed good news is ideal but can lead the experienced or the cynical to conclude that you are being economical and selective with the truth.

Most of all you should avoid prolonged silence.

Suppliers

Suppliers have two concerns about their relationship with your organisation.

1. Will you pay their bills on time or at all?

2. Will you remain a customer?

Their ideal position is to be reassured about both. But unless you control the information they use to draw conclusions they will be forced to rely on speculation, which, as I have discussed elsewhere, tends towards pessimism.

Supplier nervousness can be transmitted to others and, crucially, to credit insurers who may respond by limiting their exposure, thereby creating additional concern amongst suppliers who may ask you to pay the uninsurable balance of orders in cash on delivery.

In taking steps to preserve supplier confidence in your organisation you are addressing an audience that wants to be reassured but is often neglected when the direction of communication appears to flow towards customers, shareholders and lenders.

You should prepare a, not more than, five-point list of the key beliefs that you want suppliers to elicit from the communication they receive and bear in mind that the credibility of the message is reinforced or eroded by the organisation's behaviour in its administration. Implying that your company is financially stable while, at the same time, you fail to meet payment promises will simply compound any problems of credibility.

Make sure that your website has a specific area for supplier information and that all supplier-facing staff have a detailed and up-to-date set of likely questions and prepared answers.

Also ensure that you establish an easy, intranet based, method for supplier-facing staff to log comments and perceptions of emerging issues and give someone the task of compiling a daily analysis.

If approached properly suppliers will be helpful in managing you through turbulent times. They will be as flexible as their own problems permit. What they want from you is the continuation of your business, ideally at the current level, and for you to pay when you say you will, ideally in accordance with the contractual terms and conditions but, if some other schedule is agreed, that they receive payment when it is expected. In other words they want you to provide the consistency which contributes to their own stability.

Customers

Customers can feel similarly marginalised, like spectators who must watch the game as a series of fragments of information from mass media supplemented by rumour.

Turbulent times can cause management to take customers for granted while their attention is directed to extinguishing the immediate threats to the stability of the organisation.

The expectation that sales momentum originating in previous periods will secure revenue at expected levels, and that customers are neither part of the problem nor the solution to more pressing issues is dangerously risky thinking.

It is this somewhat careless attitude to the nurturing of the marketplace that also underpins the reduction in marketing spend as one of the first and easiest cost reduction items, as discussed more fully in chapter 12. As a result your organisation's visibility with customers declines at the time when they require reassurance that they are not taking undue risks with their business or disposable income by continuing to trade with you.

If you manage a business-to-business organisation or a big-ticket consumer business such as an airline you must implement a programme that keeps your significant and long-standing customers reassured that their interests are not being disregarded and that you understand their concerns.

There is no single initiative that will accomplish this. You must deploy a range of programmes to promote current sales and develop customer loyalty. For example, if your shares in your company are traded then it is possible that, because of the turbulent times, they stand at a relatively low price so maybe shareholders will consent to you offering loyal customers an incentive programme that pays out in options to purchase discounted shares. Customers will see this as value that they can't realise today but may be able to liquidate at a significantly higher price in the future. It is in their financial interests to divert business to you unless one of your competitors matches the programme.

In addition:

- Provide customer-facing personnel with a set of key questions and answers.

- Use media that concerned customers can access at their convenience to obtain up-to-date information.

- Install a dedicated telephone line or routing system that gives your latest press release.

- Email customers regularly with information about products, their orders and other information that keeps them 'attached' to the organisation in a way that makes them feel that they are important and valued.

Set up a page on your website that explains what is happening in your organisation and replies to any negative media speculation.

Do not let your only contact be to chase them for overdue payments or to pressure them to resolve disputed bills.

If you have a consumer-facing organisation then you must be more imaginative than simply resorting to price reductions to stimulate demand.

In a recession most retailers engage in almost permanent price promotions or sales. In some cases this is a defensive response to their competitors who were the first mover in using price reductions as their principal marketing tactic. But it is relative price that motivates consumers and if everyone reduces their price then consumers perceive no advantage to changing the way they have ranked their preference in normal times.

In turbulent times overall demand tends, at best, to remain constant and more likely will decline, especially for considered purchase items. Market shares tend to remain more or less the same as competitors are quick to neutralise any tactical advantage by matching each other's marketing initiatives.

In such conditions a few people trade up to higher priced brands now discounted to a level that they can afford and others trade down. But all sales tend to be completed at lower gross profit margins than previously and the competitive battle can reduce to a contest of who has the most robust and durable balance sheet.

I am not going to prescribe alternative marketing strategies as too much depends on the nature of your product or service, the market position of your business, your resources and the strength of your competitors.

But what I can say is that experience has revealed that there are more options to be evaluated than price reductions and that it is the innovative programmes that communicate and establish the discriminated market position that are the prerequisite for profitable marginal gains in market share.

Employees

In turbulent times all employees fear for their economic security. They know that unemployment rises and that this is a period when finding another job may not be easy and when their personal creditors such as credit card and mortgage companies are least tolerant of personal illiquidity.

Employees show signs of stress as rumours abound. Even the apparent stability of the organisation causes people to speculate on how long it can last. Every reversal can be regarded as the beginning of a bad trend, pessimism can become the predominant culture in which the failure of a competitor or major customer signals problems that will almost always lead to a cost-reduction programme which will involve redundancies.

Their fears are usually well founded. Employees disseminate information efficiently like a miniature marketplace so that often, without any formal announcement, the organisation's true situation is understood by most employees even though they may wish they are wrong and hope for something better.

It should, therefore, be clear that your employees' mood is determined by informal communication received from unofficial sources in advance of formal announcements.

Formal communication does no more than confirm and reinforce what are already widely held beliefs. There are few surprises and if management attempts to deny or fails to confirm what employees already know then credibility is lost at a crucial moment.

The manager's task is to penetrate and to control the messages circulating in the informal information system.

Most employees realise that they can have little impact on the turbulent flows that will determine their fate and for this reason they look for a leader in whom they can have faith that their interests are being looked after.

They measure anyone who positions themselves as the leader by the frequency, style and content of her/his communication as they need to believe that there is a person who epitomises the organisation's resistance to the turmoil that they see around them.

Unless they find a personification of potential salvation the stress of pessimistic speculation leads to sub-optimal performance and to a loss of organisational energy.

Managing through turbulent times necessitates increasing organisational flexibility, and flexibility is made easier as employees come to regard a different role, even one that is less desirable, as preferable to not surviving. With stressed and disengaged employees, manufacturing increased organisational flexibility is virtually impossible as the natural tendency is for each person to seek their own defensive position in which their strengths are clear and can be valued.

Change is risky and not what people want unless they perceive it as a new task that follows the restructuring programme. It becomes feasible only when a sufficient number of employees are prepared to follow a leader. Leaders are not followed because the individual occupies the principal position of authority but because followers are drawn voluntarily towards a guiding mind who may already occupy the senior position in the organisational hierarchy or comes to the position.

So on the T-matrix internal communication has the objective of preventing movement up the vertical axis and must be designed to negate pessimism, counteract rumour, and enhance organisational flexibility.

Useful methods are:

- Set up an internal website (intranet) that contains up-to-date press comments, the organisation's responses, and information about competitors. Make this someone's primary task.

- Send text messages and emails alerting employees to good news on the website.

- Be visible. Walk the building frequently. Talk to people and listen.

- Attempt to map the informal communication flows to identify the group of people who are opinion leaders and who you need to brief in order to ensure that the message is communicated with fidelity to the largest possible number of employees.

- Arrange group meetings at which the informal communication system can be nudged in the direction you prefer. Remember that the internal 'social' standing of the opinion leaders (rumour mongers if you prefer) is dependent on their being perceived by employees to retail accurate information and therefore if they know that the truth will be confirmed in a regular meeting they are less likely to embellish their story with fiction.

Job losses

In the event that it is necessary to restructure the organisation it is important that those who are to leave the organisation are treated in a humane and compassionate manner.

Managers will be diminished in the eyes of those who are to remain with the organisation if they are perceived as seeking objectionable validation of their authority by treating those whose employment they have terminated with disrespect. The status of those employees who are to leave changes, they are no longer part of the organisation's future and as a result may be regarded as being of little importance or value and are sometimes disregarded and shunned to the point of being stigmatised. This is inexcusable and indefensible and management must discourage this behaviour by setting an example to other employees and encouraging those who are to remain to participate actively in helping the leavers in any way they can.

Downsizing is an unfortunate fact of the economic system on which our society depends and, as an unwelcome process, it touches the lives of more people in turbulent times than at any other moment in the business cycle.

But it is inexcusable for managers to regard as mere units of cost the people they strived to employ and welcomed into the organisation during a previous, more buoyant phase. This is the commoditisation of labour that Karl Marx described and which we believe our moral civil society has overcome. It reveals that turbulent times can have the pernicious effect of stripping away the civilised veneer of the relationship between manager and the managed, reasserting a power relationship that owes more to the novels of Charles Dickens than to modern managerial practice.

Such behaviour or even the suspicion of it diminishes any senior manager who tolerates it in trying to establish or enhance a climate of authoritarianism at the time when cooperation is paramount. Management by coercion is never a pretty sight. It is also counterproductive.

Also, the way in which managers conduct themselves towards employees in restructuring programmes sends powerful signals to the organisation. It is a form of communication that must be managed carefully.

An example of how not to do it was given by the UK Automobile Association who on 31 January 2006 invited its patrol staff to volunteer for redundancy by the following telephone text message:

> *"£12,000 is still on offer should anyone wish to leave."*

Such a message reduces the staff to equivalent cost units of £12,000 each. There are no personalities here, no measures of competency or consideration of circumstances. No respect for or recognition of employees as individuals, just confirmation that every person is merely an identical unit of cost.

In 2003, the UK personal injury claims business The Accident Group made redundant 2,500 people after its parent company The Amulet Group filed for administration under the UK Insolvency Act. Most of these people were notified by text message to their mobile phones with a message from the administrator PwC as follows:

> *"All staff who are being retained will be contacted today. If you have not been spoken to you are therefore being made redundant with immediate effect."*

Pause for a moment to consider what your reaction would be were you to receive this message. Consider also how you would feel about working for an organisation that conducted themselves in this way.

The way in which those who are leaving the company are treated shapes the way in which those who are to remain with the organisation perceive both it and the senior manager. *If they treat these people in such an uncompassionate way to what degree can they be relied upon to act in my best interests?* This is a reasonable question for those who remain to ask.

Do not deprive people of their self-esteem at the moment they need it most. Treat people as individuals not groups or stereotypes. Give them your time and help.

Let's explore some of the positive messages that can be communicated by undertaking these conspicuous exercises more compassionately.

- You all realise that these are turbulent times and that as an organisation we are not immune to them.

- The organisation has encountered difficulties.

- We believe that together we can overcome these problems.

- But to do so we need to reorganise and unfortunately that means that we cannot afford to continue to employ everyone.

- To minimise compulsory layoffs we have instigated the following:

    - A programme of job-sharing for a period of six months in which those of you who are able to participate will continue to be employed but at 60% of your previous salary.

    - All management salaries are to be reduced for an initial period of six months so that two managers will effectively subsidise the job of a lower paid employee for that period.

    - For those of you who wish to leave there will be a programme of voluntary redundancy.

- We intend to reduce production by closing plants for an extended holiday period for which employees will be paid 60% of their earnings.

Eventually you will reach the position at which the turbulence abates and the future becomes clearer. Make sure that you inform employees of this. The message, *"its over and together we have survived"* is a powerful platform from which to develop plans for the future.

10

Planning for the present

Management practice in stable times is analogous to taking a journey. Objectives are set in the form of budgets and plans and intermediate points are specified at which measures of progress are taken. This is like following a map and recognising landmarks along the way.

However, in turbulent times the map becomes useless as the previously surveyed landscape begins to change in unpredictable ways.

The options facing managers are:

1.   Carry on regardless.

2.   Retrace your steps in the hope of finding known territory.

3.   Seek guidance about the route ahead.

Few people are prepared to carry on into the unknown if they do not feel equipped or sufficiently flexible to adapt to a wide range of possible conditions.

A substantial number will stop and seek information about the conditions ahead, find a guide or someone from whom they can obtain an up-to-date map. Their decision about whether to proceed or retreat will depend on how confident they feel having collected this new information.

A large fraction will identify retreat as the least risky option and retrace their steps (let's get back to basics) in the expectation that they will find a familiar environment in which they feel secure.

But retracing your steps is a false offer of security as it is hardly ever possible to reverse course. You cannot time travel into the past or recreate the previous conditions in the present. The world moves on and attempts to re-access an antecedent state are no less risky than riding the wave of turbulence into an unknown future.

Planning for the present requires adoption of a mode of coping. The future is unknown and the problems that may emerge in the present are unpredictable. So the rational objective is to ensure that your business survives the turbulence and that means you have to be prepared to alter course rapidly as the turmoil unfolds and exposes your organisation to unexpected challenges and risks.

Whether you emerge as a healthy or disabled survivor depends on the degree of your adaptability and the severity of the turmoil you encounter. The more flexible your business model and the more adaptable your managerial team the greater the chance of emerging as a healthy survivor.

As survival assumes a pre-eminent position the planning horizon shrinks. Planning must become focussed on *being* and only be concerned with *becoming* when it is clear what can be preserved and what must be detached, abandoned or restructured to ensure viability over the medium term.

In this context the present has two active components:

1. Generating sufficient cash in this period to cover the costs in the next period.

2. Achieving the best possible position at the point that the turbulent times end.

Point '1' needs little additional comment. Point '2' is a more challenging exercise.

The 2008 book *Business Planning in Turbulent Times; new methods for applying scenarios,*[16] provides some valuable insights. Rafael Ramirez, one of the authors, places planning in such conditions in perspective with the following statement:

---

[16] *Business Planning in Turbulent Times* by Rafael Ramirez, Jon W Selsky and Kees van der Heijden, Earthscan (2008).

"In a turbulent world, successful leaders are less like those who know where they want to take us, than those who can help us prepare for different circumstances."[17]

The book is about scenario planning which is an alternative methodology that will help you to formulate a range of models of the possible conditions that may prevail when the turbulence ends and how these might develop.

You need to begin with a realistic appraisal of your current position and how it will develop over the next 6 to 12 months. Additionally you need to consider a range of answers to the following:

a. The duration of the turbulence.

b. The degree of turbulence that will be encountered before conditions improve.

c. The degree to which your organisation will be effected by a and b.

d. Where you would ideally wish to be positioned at the end of phase IV of the credit cycle (see page 264).

The important output information is:

a. The extent of the restructuring you need to undertake, its cost and the resources you need to acquire in order to reposition to your most desirable position.

b. The position you are able to achieve using the resources you feel that you are able to acquire and its viability.

It is psychologically difficult to adjust the thinking of a managerial team that has become used to managing the present in accordance with a plan for the future and to deprive them of the orientation provided by

---

[17]

www.sbs.ox.ac.uk/news/archives/Undergraduate/Managing+in+turbulent+times.htm

this longer-term objective. A vision of survival seems less attractive than one of progress.

A further danger is to concede too readily, in order to minimise discord, to the pressure exerted on the most senior manager by other members of the team who, for a short period, understand the need for a coping strategy but too quickly agitate to reintroduce longer-term objectives. In part they regard doing so as symbolic that the organisation has done what is necessary to ensure survival and can now resume a path of progress. These individuals perceive opportunities offered by the potential weakness of competitors and are concerned not to weaken the competitive position of your business and allow competitors to cure their difficulties because you failed to defend what has been built over the preceding period.

But you must ensure that everyone is clear that the principal organisational objective is to endure and the subordinate goal is to emerge as a healthy survivor. Only when it is absolutely clear that the principal objective is assured can you turn to planning beyond the present and to expanding your horizon of expectation.

Competitive strategy

In turbulent times it is very easy to become so absorbed by your own problems that you neglect the effect that general problems, such as recession, will have on your customers and competitors.

In persistent uncertainty there is an understandable desire to find things on which you can rely. You measure the movement of your organisation by reference to customers and competitors. Gaining customers that have previously been loyal to your competitor boosts confidence. Losing your customers to them can damage your confidence disproportionately. The managerial psychology that prevails in turbulent times has a tendency to exaggerate negative changes and underweight the benefit of positive events.

This pessimistic asymmetry can accelerate the decline of an organisation and present a difficult communication and motivation task for senior management.

You must take care in assuming that your reading of the market will remain constant when your initiatives become visible. For example, the natural response of many mangers to falling sales is to reduce prices in the belief that this will both attract new customers and will discourage existing customers from being tempted away by the offers of others.

In turbulent times it is probable that one of your competitors will be unable to resist the temptation to reduce prices to stimulate demand or gain market share. You will then come under pressure both internally and from customers to match these price cuts in order to restore the relative balance within the market.

If consumer behaviour is influenced significantly or only by price then, by matching each others price movements, the consequence will tend to be that, all other things being equal, market shares will stay the same but gross profit will diminish. More creative competitive strategies are required, one of which may be to accept a reduction in sales to preserve gross profit at a level higher than it would otherwise have been (see chapter 12, Downsizing).

If the turbulence you are confronting is exclusive to you, such as:

- Difficult acquisition integration.

- Resolving an inappropriate financial structure.

- Plant closure problem or product recall issue causing a loss of production or confidence.

Then you must be aware of the vulnerabilities created and how your competitors will seek to take advantage and make plans to counteract each potential move against you.

You must not construct your plans for the present without thinking through your competitive strategy in detail and the greatest danger to avoid is to assume that your competitors are experiencing less turbulence than you.

At a time when all the variables in the complex equation seem to be moving simultaneously and in unpredictable ways there is a natural tendency to simplify the task of interpretation by holding constant those that are beyond your direct control. But this is an error because it detaches your volatility from that of the market and thereby causes you to proceed on the basis of a false understanding of cause and effect.

Turbulence is complexity and attempts to simplify do not reduce the turbulence but simply misrepresent what is actually happening. That is why the conventional arithmetic method of planning and evaluating competitive strategy should be subordinated to the concept of scenario planning.

11

Managing the balance sheet

Cash is more important than profit

In times of economic hardship lenders and advisers always encourage management to focus on cash generation. They are correct. In these conditions credit becomes tight and comparatively expensive and therefore there is less capacity for management to bridge short-term liquidity problems with additional borrowings.

Many solvent companies have failed because they are illiquid and unable to raise additional finance because lenders will not subordinate or share their existing collateral interests, and possible new lenders see the additional facilities as high risk if they are in a senior position and too high a risk if they are subordinated.

So what more, you may ask, needs to be said other than to pose the question, what action can I take to generate cash and accelerate cash flow?

Well, let me explain why you must be smart about the cash you generate otherwise your success may lead you into greater problems than those you thought enhanced cash generation would cure.

If your company has exhibited or your bankers suspect that you may be experiencing trading difficulties, technically referred to in loan agreements as material adverse change in either actual or prospective condition of the business, then, at the time when you notify them of your success in converting assets to cash, in order to force you to apply the cash to a reduction in their exposure they may then seek opportunities to declare actual or anticipatory default.

By doing this they manage their balance sheet by first using your cash to convert a loan asset into cash which, in turbulent times, is a better quality of asset to have on the bank's balance sheet as it is risk-free and therefore reduces their overall risk profile.

You may protest that by capping your loan facilities at a lower level the bank is eliminating your financial flexibility to the point at which you are uncertain of your ability to deal with the unexpected events that may arise as a result of the turbulent conditions. This may be interpreted as your business being potentially unstable.

The bank may then re-examine the remaining assets that comprise their collateral and conclude that your programme of successful cash generation has depleted the high-quality assets, leaving their residual exposure secured against a pool of less desirable assets that, if they had to foreclose and liquidate, will leave them with a greater percentage loss.

Also, by forcing you to reduce borrowing they may move you to a higher risk category of debtor or from a medium-sized account to a small account. Each bank classifies accounts in this way and adopts a different policy towards members of each group that encounter problems.

You may be asked to provide additional collateral and to accept an increase in the bank's charges to reflect the greater risk.

Often, borrowers of comparatively small amounts, say up to GBP 10mm, are, in turbulent times, regarded as more trouble to manage than they are worth. The lender prefers to apply its limited resources to large distressed borrowers and may therefore elect to foreclose in the event of actual or anticipatory default, take the hit against provisions and move on to the next case.

Additionally, lenders may be cognisant that loans are credit insured and may find that the insurance only pays out in the event of a formal bankruptcy procedure being instigated. In such cases the lender may elect for an early foreclosure in order to claim the insured sum.

Banks don't care about your business. They know that in the next credit cycle there will be other lending opportunities with which to replace your business.

They also regard as questionable any management team that comes to them and declares problems, and in a climate of turbulence they do not want to support management in which they have less than 100% confidence.

After all, this management has just given the bankers another problem that they did not anticipate and do not appreciate. Hence, negotiation and confrontation become the psychological states of both parties.

When, in the good times, lenders say that they want a close business relationship to help your company develop, what they actually mean is that they would like to penetrate your business deeply so that they can identify additional opportunities.

What they do not mean is that they will be tolerant and understanding of management that fails to protect the bank's interests from impairment in turbulent times.

In stable times banks want to be a part of your success. In turbulent times they demand that you operate your business to protect them from the threats to their economic wellbeing.

You may think that this is a cynical view of lenders. Certainly, few would acknowledge it openly. But it is the way they behave and it is rational and understandable.

Banks and other lending institutions are just like your company. They suffer in turbulent times and the source of their difficulties is the same clients that they courted in the good times, whose financial problems are also the lenders' problems.

Whatever action the lender can take to resolve its problem must affect your company and so corporate management comes to regard the lender as an additional destabilising factor.

With both parties regarding the other as the origin of at least some of their problems it is not surprising that confrontation and a power struggle can develop.

Corporate management will invite trouble if it fails to understand that, in turbulent times, their lender is not a supportive friend seeking to solve a common problem but an adversary intent primarily on self-protection.

This is not materially different to the stance you take with defaulting debtors. You were delighted to win their business but now that they refuse to pay you regard their intransigence as an act of betrayal.

So why bother generating cash?

If generating cash can make you an attractive target for predatory lenders you might ask why bother? Surely it would be better to just generate enough to pay the next period's costs.

In turbulent times there are enhanced risks in your receivables and inventory and it is preferable to convert as much as possible into cash as quickly as possible.

It is important to remember that today's action to generate cash is intended to pay tomorrow's costs and the cash you realise today determines the costs you are able to afford tomorrow. Hence, cash flow will set the horizon of security for the business and the more distant this is the more stable the company.

The objective is to retain the cash for use within the company and you must plan the use of funds at the same time as you plan cash generation.

The greatest risk to your cash arises if you hold significant balances in excess of your normal monthly requirements.

This is less of a problem if your treasury arrangements and debt covenants do not require you to report your balances to lenders so you are able to maintain the cash in an account with a non-lending institution.

But given that most lenders will be seeking surplus cash residing in their borrowers you must be cautious in trying to conceal your cash balances, as lenders may identify a reduction in your average receivables or inventory while your creditors are unchanged and realise that you have converted assets into unutilised cash.

As today's cash has no other purpose but to fund tomorrow's costs you should plan to use the cash to negotiate a reduction in future costs by prepaying some and seeking additional discounts for accelerated payment of others.

For example, discuss with your landlord the discount he will offer if you pay the next 12 months rent in advance. Utility companies will discount if you place a deposit against future consumption or discuss buying futures contracts for energy and raw materials. Consider buying raw materials in advance on behalf of your suppliers.

Your objective in formulating a use of cash plan must be to reduce future costs and maximise the horizon of security in which the company can operate stably.

Lenders may be frustrated by this change in your business model but they will get over it and in the process come to regard you as proficient managers who have created a period of stability where others tried to manage turbulence.

How to generate cash

One-off cash generation programme – find the locked away cash

In every company there is a store of frozen cash. It exists in excess inventories, waste material, unused and discarded assets including office equipment, unbilled work in progress, prepayments, unsettled litigation, etc.

The first task is to identify each of these items and instigate a programme to turn them into cash immediately. You must evaluate the write-downs that this may entail and whether these will lead to issues with lenders who have a collateral interest in the value of the assets.

Often having someone walk around each building with the specific brief to list and question the retention of anything that is lying idle will yield a significant amount of frozen cash.

Aim to retain only those assets that are productive and liquidate the others by any means, even through unconventional markets such as eBay.

Dealing with inventory

If you do not already do so attempt to relate the value of inventory to the revenue/gross profit.

For example, you may be able to conclude that 10% of raw material relates to 40% of revenue and therefore that 90% of your inventory is supporting only 60% of your revenue and take steps to adjust the balance and, as a result, release cash.

Perhaps analysis also reveals that 80% of finished goods inventory relates to 20% of revenue pa.

You should set clear targets for increasing the inventory turnover per annum and generate cash from this to increase the velocity of circulation of a smaller amount of working capital locked in inventory.

Dealing with debtors

In a time of general turbulence most people slow down their bill payment as they attempt to conserve cash. You will probably do the same but paradoxically think that your customers are acting unreasonably by paying you later than normal.

If you are relaxed in your receivable management and allow customers to take longer they will exploit this opportunity to its fullest. It will be difficult for you to recover the situation and return to a more disciplined schedule of prompt payment without incurring some bad feeling with your customer that may extend beyond the period of turbulence.

So it is preferable not to let payment cycles fall out of control in the first place.

This will be easier to accomplish if you are a key supplier than if you are marginal or provide services and equipment as part of a capital project that is about to be terminated or mothballed as an economy measure.

As part of the programme to thaw frozen cash all receivables that are overdue should be examined at least weekly by senior management. Each account in arrears should be assigned to someone who is given the responsibility of clearing the arrears and incentivised accordingly.

A number of actions can be taken to accomplish this, including:

- Ensure that the account balance in arrears doesn't grow. Each new bill should be confirmed as acceptable before it is due and the customer asked for a payment date.

- Account limits should be set that necessitate the overdue balance being reduced on a monthly schedule. Customers requiring new goods that would cause the balance to exceed the limit should be asked to pay in cash on receipt for the excess amount.

- When an invoice remains unpaid because there is some dispute try to establish the fraction that is *not* in dispute and credit the value of the disputed element and re-invoice this. The debtor then has no reason to withhold the undisputed balance.

- Avoid issuing single bills with substantial values. Break invoicing down into small amounts to avoid the temptation of retaining a substantial sum by finding a dispute on a single invoice.

- Offer an early payment and prompt payment discount that equals the time-adjusted value of cash to you.

- If customers remain intransigent then use legal processes to recover the amount owed. Most countries have a method to enforce payment more rapidly than engaging in conventional civil litigation. In the UK you can issue a statutory demand[18] that starts a count down of 21 days in which the debt must be paid or the demand set aside by the court otherwise the demand leads to the issuing of a winding up order against the debtor if they ignore the proceedings.

---

[18] Sections 123 (1) a, 222 (1) a or 268 (1) a of the Insolvency Act 1986.

- Small companies with large companies as debtors can use this process with great effect as large organisations may pay rather than take the risk of failing to adhere to the strict process due to administrative inefficiency.

- Consider selling bundles of small overdue invoices to specialist collection agencies (non-recourse invoice discounting) at a discount to their face value. Yes you may take a hit on the balance sheet but you will receive cash quickly without involving costly and scarce internal resources that can be deployed to greater effect on other tasks.

- Ask your lawyers to report on retention of title provisions. If your conditions of sale contain this clause then you need to understand how you can enforce this. Are you able to identify the specific goods over which you retain title? What action is available to you if the goods have been sold on or incorporated as a component in another product?

- If you are engaged in a downsizing process which involves deciding which accounts you may close make sure you feed the payment record into the process. With some customers it may be worthwhile to explain that they are being assessed as part of this programme and the fact that their account is in arrears may move them into the questionable relationship category. If you are an important supplier the customer is likely to rectify the problem quickly.

- Credit insurance may be difficult to obtain for a debtor who is already seriously in arrears and you can use this to change the terms of trade.

- One of the toughest decisions is whether to continue to trade with a company for whom credit insurance is withdrawn. This is the reason why many companies and especially retailers fail. The underwriters withdraw coverage and suppliers are not prepared to take the credit risk, so trading cannot continue and the business collapses.

There is no easy answer to these situations as much depends on the stability of the customer, their capacity to offer some alternative security for payment and the importance of their business to your company.

Dealing with creditors (including lenders)

No creditor wants to receive the bad news that your organisation is likely to be in default as this information adds to their level of turbulence. In turbulent times lenders are a category of creditor that is particularly sensitive to your organisation's financial condition. They realise that default will be a more frequent occurrence and take steps to manage their exposure so they will be prepared for your bad news and will have established procedures to handle the situation to their advantage. They may therefore be better prepared than you and begin to dictate your agenda.

Other creditors may have less contractual capacity to destabilise your business but, nonetheless, they cannot be treated in a dismissive or arrogant manner because you believe they need your business and will therefore tolerate whatever action you impose to improve your position.

It is too easy to delay payment thereby transferring some of your financial problem onto your creditors. Certainly you will find that some may be able to tolerate you taking longer to pay whereas others, perhaps even important suppliers, will not.

By imposing variations in terms without negotiation at an individual level you risk disrupting inputs to your business and, potentially, damaging relationships that may become crucial if you are to prosper when the upturn arrives.

In summary the lessons from previous recessions are:

- Be careful with those on whom you are dependent.

- In multi-bank negotiations, covenant tests, stand still agreements, etc., take time to understand the lender's position.

- If you are borrowing in different jurisdictions understand the differences between the legal frameworks that determine what lenders can and cannot do and the timescales.

- Take whatever discounts are available from creditors for early or prompt payment. Consider this to be a good use of the surplus cash generated by releasing frozen cash.

- In case creditors refuse to supply or collapse ensure that you have emergency sourcing plans for crucial components etc.

- If there is a danger of supplier instability and you feel it is prudent to increase buffer stocks, can you arrange this to be at the cost of the supplier?

- Review all contracts to understand the clauses that may be used to destabilise your company but also any ways in which you can negotiate better terms.

In practical terms this means:

- Not believing that lenders or insurers will support you if you encounter problems.

- Making sure your suppliers do not transfer their problems to you by imposing price increases and varying payment terms.

- Negotiating with each significant supplier on an individual basis rather than imposing general policy initiatives.

- Creating low inventories but rapid call off of new goods. The flexibility you desire must extend to your suppliers and logistics.

- Not filling your distribution pipeline with goods that are slow to sell and therefore restrict revenues in future periods.

- Possibly limiting your product portfolio to only the fastest moving goods and those that can be supplied most quickly.

- In service companies the same process applies only you need to narrow your list of services or their geographical reach, which may mean reducing the permanent head count and shrinking the business.

- In all businesses it means identifying rapidly the areas in which your competitors are re-shaping their portfolios and determining in negotiation with suppliers whether this offers you an opportunity to enter this segment with scale and at increased margin. Even if this was a segment you abandoned recently.

- It means closing down all projects that consume cash or other resources that minimise flexibility.

- It means directing resources to the maximisation of flexibility and understanding which suppliers are inflexible.

- It means investing in customer loyalty and lock-in schemes that reward customers who stay with you for at least 2 years and getting creditors to contribute to the cost as success benefits them.

Dealing with shareholders

How you deal with shareholders depends on whether you are a private or a public company and the distribution of the shares. Are there just a few major shareholders or many small shareholders?

For public companies the conditions of listing on the stock exchange dictate the points at which information that may be price sensitive must be revealed and consequently management is constrained from exercising any inclination they might have to conceal bad news.

In private companies the shareholders tend to be a closer group and management is under no obligation not to delay informing them of bad news.

In both public and private companies the maintenance of dividends is often regarded by management as a key signal that the company is OK. You may be forced to issue a profit warning but if you say nothing about reducing or stopping dividend payments the interpretation may be that management does not perceive the situation to be more than a temporary blip.

Management's confidence in the future may or may not be misplaced but shareholders obviously prefer to secure a future for the company rather than see the business collapse because management continued to pay dividends when the better call was to explain to shareholders that turbulent times, which they will understand, means that the company must conserve its financial resources until the outturn is clear.

Of course shareholders will prefer that the value of their investment did not decline and that their dividend stream continues, but they look to management for reassurance and are seriously and rightly disturbed to learn that the managers, in whose hands they placed their financial wellbeing, have failed to act in their best interests.

When public companies suddenly collapse or encounter very severe difficulties you hear shareholders ask:

> *Why did management not see the problems coming? And if they did, why didn't they warn us?*

Failure of management's initial policies of denial and concealment rarely leaves a good platform on which to engage with shareholders, especially if the next step is to ask the same shareholders to invest new money to support the incumbent management.

Informed shareholders may still be disappointed but are more likely to be supportive than those who learn that they have been 'kept in the dark' until management could no longer deny, conceal or contain the bad news which is now received as a shock.

Throughout this book I suggest that turbulent times require managers to be more expansive in their thought processes and not to dismiss counterintuitive options.

This also applies to their dealings with shareholders. For example, managers may feel that issuing a profit warning is a negative step to be resisted unless it becomes unavoidable. It is certainly not positive news but shareholders are not stupid and they understand that few companies are totally immune to the negative impact of adverse economic conditions.

Silence leads to speculation, which in turbulent times is mostly negative and results in people selling their shares which signals to others that they should do likewise because someone in the community of sellers will be trading on the basis of information that may not be in the public arena. Consequently, issuing a profit warning can fill the void of silence that otherwise can invite the conjecture that the impact on the company must be severe otherwise management would have made a reassuring statement when the share price began to fall. The profit warning may not be as negative as the speculation and hence the situation can be 'spun' to be moderately positive.

Receiving a profit warning is not good news but it is news and suggests that management is not in denial or engaging in misplaced optimism, which is toxically dangerous in turbulent times. Additionally, it provides some guidance as to the magnitude of the impact, which can reassure shareholders that management is facing up to the problems and taking appropriate precautions.

It is managing expectations.

Let me cite an example for the UK.

Northern Rock Plc was the casualty that provided the overture to the financial crisis in the UK.

Between December 2002 and June 2007 Northern Rock increased its assets from GBP 42bn to GBP 113bn. The GBP 71bn increase was financed mainly by additional debt sourced from the interbank market.

In the half-year statement dated 27 July 2007 the bank's CEO stated:

"The medium term outlook of the company is very positive."

Six weeks later he announced that the Bank of England had agreed to inject emergency funds as the lender of last resort.

How can this July statement be reconciled with the rapid collapse into the arms of the Bank of England which culminated in Northern Rock being nationalised? Management argued that they never anticipated the unprecedented (not since the late 1920's) illiquidity in the interbank market, which meant they could not refinance maturing short-term loan facilities.

On reflection, that Northern Rock's dependence on the interbank market could lead to this crisis was clear to anyone who cared to look. It should have been apparent to the UK regulator of banks (the FSA) that Northern Rock's business model placed it, like all highly leveraged businesses, in a position of acute vulnerability to the inaccessibility of bank borrowing, even over the short run.

It was clear that the credit cycle was in its final phase and, importantly, that it had been extended artificially and allowed to develop in a unprecedented form by the deliberate dampening of the economic contraction and adjustment that should have arisen naturally around the turn of the millennium.

For Northern Rock to have acknowledged publicly that the credit cycle was entering a disadvantageous phase at a time of significant debt financed expansion would, of course, have been to call into question its own business model. To change the business model would send unwelcome signals to lenders and investors so, as in many examples of corporate instability, the management appeared to deny and later conceal their fears in the hope that the storm would pass without consequence.

It didn't and the bank collapsed. Northern Rock's demise is not unique. There is a similar level of intransigence present in the collapse of Lehman. But could another approach have avoided this? With the benefit of hindsight management could have realised their vulnerability and taken steps over the preceding year to refinance their short-term facilities with longer-term loans that matched funding to the length of their lending to mortgage customers, but their superior profits would have been reduced. Shareholders might even have found a call for further capital to underpin the bank's rapid growth reasonable.

In the case of both Northern Rock and Lehman by following the path they had taken to success, they found failure.

They are not alone.

Shareholders of Northern Rock lost most of their investment in the nationalisation programme and most would have been happier to have enjoyed lower returns for a few years but retain their interest in a business that resumed its growth when conditions improved.

My conclusion is that managers should resist the temptation to regard shareholders as a fan club that you milk for funds and applause in the good times but treat as alien predators when you fear that turbulent times mean that you have to inform them that the trend of previous years cannot be sustained.

Most worthwhile shareholders are there for the long run and if they believe that the fundamentals of your business are sound they will play their part in helping you to ride out the storm.

Even if your share register is dominated by shareholders who are noted for their short-term attitude, it is pointless trying to disguise the situation. They expect you to say something so silence and half-truths will not suffice.

Your plan must be to actively manage your share register and shareholders' expectations in order to move short-term holdings into the hands of institutions that take a longer view.

You must regard this activity as part of the general programme of creating stability by converting as many short-term positions, associations and contracts as possible into medium and long-term forms.

12

Downsizing

There are several euphemisms used to describe the deliberate contraction of the business. Downsizing, rightsizing, restructuring, rationalisation are some of them used frequently.

Whatever name you attach to the process the programme objective is to establish a new balance between revenue, margins and costs.

In most companies the effects of economic turbulence are experienced financially and the instinctive response is to reduce costs and increase margins but not to increase revenues.

Usually, a target cost saving is set and a plan formulated for how the company can be downsized to operate at this lower level of fixed cost.

Before we move to a detailed discussion about downsizing and cost-cutting I want to emphasise something of critical importance.

I believe that for the company to avoid multiple periods of cost-cutting during turbulent times is not just idealistic but psychologically important and worth striving for, especially in announcing lay-offs.

There is nothing more unsettling for employees and other stakeholders than to experience a series of downsizing initiatives. There is nothing more motivating than to be told that this is the only programme of lay-offs and that you are one of the people chosen to be retained because we believe you can make the restructured business work.

Of course things change and my persistent theme about building organisational flexibility is predicated on this as an expectation. Hence, it is sometimes necessary to respond to unexpected events by changing the shape of the organisation more than once, but this should be because there has been a recognisable additional event and not because the initial downsizing was inadequate or misconceived.

It is not unusual for a company that encounters difficulties in turbulent times to formulate and finance a downsizing plan to address them, but for the plan to fail to deliver the expected benefits according to the time schedule. It is this failure to deliver that moves managers from the mode of negotiation to confrontation.

It is unusual, if they remain in position, for the same managers to avoid creating a severely disabled survivor and often averting collapse is then beyond them.

Restructuring the organisation may be unavoidable and the point at which it is undertaken and the way it is executed will determine the condition in which the business emerges from turbulent times.

Reducing costs

Cost-cutting is often necessary but it is rarely sufficient to restore stability. This is because it is not usually possible to cut the fixed cost base of a company and to preserve its operational capability at the current level. To find some point of equilibrium between reduced costs and lower revenue often necessitates a reduction in scale to a level that is insufficient to support sunk costs and indebtedness.

The problem is to determine at what level the loss of revenue will stabilise and the danger to avoid is that cost reductions are continually chasing declining revenue.

Insufficient restructuring can lead to a downward spiral of instability. On the other hand cutting fixed costs by too great an amount may also damage the business by making it incapable of operating efficiently.

Cutting costs recently added should not be regarded as a kind of corporate time travel that enables a business or any type of organisation to move backwards along its lifespan. Downsizing moves the organisation to a new position and cannot restore an earlier stage of viability when costs were less.

In this over-simplified illustration a retail business may decide that it needs to cut costs to enlarge margins and to achieve this it will reduce inventory, store headcount and its marketing spend.

The consequence is that after an initial period customers drift away because their shopping experience deteriorates as they cannot find the range of goods that supported the proposition that attracted them in the first place and the in-store service levels are now poor and irritatingly slow. Reduced marketing spend causes the business to diminish in visibility, and at the same time that the store proposition is dissatisfying to previously loyal customers new customers are not being attracted in sufficient numbers to compensate.

Margins may seem better in the short run but declining revenue eventually creates a shortfall in gross profit, which may mean that, in the medium term, the business is worse off in cash terms.

So how do you find the right balance between cost reduction and viability?

These are the key projects that management must evaluate:

a. Maintaining marketing spend

b. Reducing headcount

c. Reducing revenue

d. Increasing margins

e. Maintaining capital and development expenditure

There is nothing wrong with reducing the scale of the business to a smaller more profitable core that will require a lower fixed cost base. You will notice that this statement implies that the question, *what is the appropriate scale?* should be answered before the question, *by how much can we cut our costs?*

But more often the question takes the form of, *by how much can we cut costs and maintain the current business model?*

What is considered less frequently is that the better solution might be to *deliberately* reduce revenue perhaps in excess of the decline predicted by a continuation of recent trends and changing to a different business model.

In turbulent times the portfolio of customers must be examined in detail to establish rankings by the following:

- Revenue

- Number of products x revenue

- GP delivery x product

- Cash delivery adjusted for the time cost[19]

- The solvency risk of each customer x GP delivery[20]

Management must then use these data to establish several scenarios created by various business shapes:

- What will be the cash outcome if one or more product ranges are terminated?

- What will be the cash outcome if the product range is maintained but contracts with low GP generating customers are terminated unless GP increases can be negotiated?

For each scenario:

- What is the cost reduction that follows naturally by reducing production, inventory, sales force and does this reveal some level of diminished scale that is sufficiently cash generative to rectify any current or anticipated liquidity issues?

---

[19] By which I mean each unit of cash must be discounted by the cost of borrowing to fund the time taken to pay.

[20] What is the risk of each customer encountering financial distress and being unable to pay on the due date or, in a worst case, filing for bankruptcy? Being insured against a loss if the customer collapses is useful, maybe crucial, but there is the broader point of what happens to the business if this gross profit is suddenly unavailable.

Maintaining marketing spend

Lord Leverhulme[21] made the intriguing and somewhat irritating statement that:

> *"half the money I spend on advertising is wasted, the trouble is I don't know which half."*

Here is the still unresolved problem of the marketing budget. Without there being an identifiable causal relationship between the change in spend and a change in revenue everyone 'feels' that this is an expenditure that can be reduced easily.

At a time of declining sales it is often claimed that marketing spend cannot be maintained at its absolute level as it would then represent a higher percentage of sales value and that, at most, it should be maintained at the same percentage. But this is not a rational argument. The causal connection between marketing spend and sales value cannot be reduced to a fixed percentage relationship. If it could this argument would remain invalid as it implies that sales create marketing spend rather than the reverse.

CFOs ask marketing management to quantify and justify the results of halving the marketing spend for 6 months or 12 months and to 'disprove' that a resumption in expenditure levels after 12 months will not rectify any temporary shortfall.

The presumption, probable correct, is that there is a lag between the reduction of marketing spend and a decline in market share. Hence, a short-term profit increase results so long as the market volume is not declining at a faster rate.

---

[21] William Hesketh Lever 1st Viscount Leverhulme (1851-1925) founder of Lever Brothers now part of Unilever.

The second assumption is that, in the future, a resumption in spend will have a more immediate effect in increasing sales and return the business to its previous scale.

But if the second proposition is true and customers are rapidly and positively influenced by marketing activity then there is also an argument that the current shortfall in revenue could be rectified by *increasing* marketing spend.

But if these rules applied to your business then they also apply to your competitors.

I cannot offer you a universally applicable rule that determines whether or not to cut your marketing budget. I understand the attraction of cutting this budget. It is a cost reduction that can be implemented quickly, probably without direct cost, or in terms of human resources issues, no-one can present a compelling case for not doing so and the argument in favour of increasing marketing spend is usually never made.

But I do counsel caution in decimating the marketing budget as the true costs in terms of damaging the business base and closing down options for 'becoming', although obscure, may be pernicious.

Of course, stability in the short run is paramount but managers must not ignore the condition in which the business emerges from turbulent times. If you are dependent upon the saliency of a brand then you must take care not to undermine its position in the short term in the mistaken belief that 'normal' conditions will resume once the turbulence has passed.

I think the simple analogy is that you can't go fishing without a hook and you cannot expect the fish to continue to jump into your basket because that's where fish have tended to be found in the past.

Reducing headcount

The most emotionally difficult form of cost reduction is to reduce headcount.

It is rarely the case that the company has been operating with surplus staff that it can let go in turbulent times without any effect on the scale of the business.

I was appointed to a substantial telecoms business that had been recently acquired for GBP 1.5bn by a larger multinational, the management of which imposed their matrix management structure with many members of staff reporting operationally to someone in the UK and functionally to someone else located in the UK but also reporting to a manager in the US. The result was that the controlled balance between revenue and headcount was lost and the number of employees doubled within 18 months. Profitability declined, cash flow turned negative and the parent began to panic that their very conspicuous acquisition was going badly wrong.

The obvious solution was to cut the headcount back to the level as at the date of acquisition, but the increased numbers had formed into a new operating structure that needed to be changed if the business was not going to collapse.

Orthodox thinking accepts that systems create the demand for new employees, but what is often ignored is that new employees also tend to add complexity which, in turn, requires additional people to manage as a new system evolves.

In the example above the company's second plan was to ask one of the major management consultancies to evaluate how employees spread their time across a large product portfolio to determine which products could be eliminated to reduce the headcount to the desired level with the smallest damage to revenue. The conclusion, not surprisingly, was that in theory revenue could be balanced with a reduced headcount at a level that was profitable, but I found that, practically, it was impossible to identify a discrete group of employees related to a specific list of products. The network had become so complex as a result of the matrix management that most employees spread their time across several products. Consequently, unless a new organisational structure was adopted by dismantling the matrix management system the headcount could not be reduced significantly without risking a collapse in revenue and gross profit to a level at which losses would be fixed.

The solution was to divide the operation into the organisation required to service the core international business and the residual national activity that was of less interest to the globally oriented parent. The current profitability and prospects of each notional business could be appraised and the cost base necessary to maintain each more easily defined. The residual costs, those that fitted neither notional business unit, could be evaluated for their relevance. This revealed:

- A group of relatively highly paid employees who were not essential to either business unit and were related to the imposition of a more complex management structure.

- A group of products that were not essential to the proposition of either business unit but existed only because the technology made them possible, they could be offered so they must be offered, or because competitors offered them.

- That much of the local (non-international) business was unprofitable because the network that supported it was incomplete.

- That the investment required to complete the local network was greater than the company could afford or could justify in the prevailing climate.

It became clear that the way forward was to consolidate the business by shrinking the operation to service international clients and preserve the local network only to the extent that it was required by these clients.

The reorganisation cost around GBP 90mm to restructure and to shrink the company to a profitable core by eliminating non-international products and the associated investment programme, reduce the related headcount, rationalise from 13 locations to 3, and remove those employees whose function arose only as a consequence of the matrix management structure.

The plan did not abandon the incomplete network and associated products but simply mothballed the infrastructure so that the business case for further investment could be re-evaluated at a future date.

In an earlier section I discussed the desirability of treating with respect and compassion those individuals who are to leave the company.

Certainly, for some managers redundancy programmes are treated as an opportunity to exhibit their authority and capacity to take tough decisions and they use the opportunity to demonstrate their dispassion in order to reinforce their coercive capacity over those who are not leaving. Such testosterone conditioned management (not confined to men) is never justifiable but, more significantly, it is counterproductive.

A good manager does not want to lose good people and behaving less than compassionately towards those who must leave the company sends a negative message to those on whose application and loyalty the company will depend.

Who wants to work for a company that allows its managers to treat people in such an unnecessarily disrespectful way? The good people will take the first opportunity to leave.

Who will accept a job offer from a company that has a recent history of behaving so badly towards its employees? Actions in turbulent times will echo in the stable phase that follows.

You must also consider the extent to which executing a headcount reduction insensitively at this time will prejudice your capacity to re-acquire the same skill-set when conditions improve.

Before you settle too rapidly on laying off large numbers of people explore whether you can use more creative approaches.

For example, if you need to reduce production to reflect high inventory of finished goods and reduced demand consider talking to unions or employee committees about closing plants for 6 months and giving the workforce a 6 month holiday on reduced pay.

Offer voluntary redundancy packages to anyone who feels unable to accept the enforced vacation and temporary income reduction.

If you need to keep some production operating but at a lower level than normal explore job sharing amongst existing staff.

Consider deferring a portion of wages and salaries until the turbulent times pass. Maybe offer to pay a portion of wages and salaries in new shares so that employees have an opportunity to gain more money in the future than they have deferred in the current phase.

To show employees that the downsizing is not the sacrifice of the jobs of many to maintain the high incomes of a few, consider asking senior managers to subsidise one or several employees that you would ideally like to retain by reducing their own salary by a sum equivalent to the employee's pay.

Consolidating plants is an established device, not only for reducing headcount but also for trimming inventories and improving productivity. Attractive as this may be, large-scale physical reorganisation is expensive and disruptive and, normally, cannot be undertaken rapidly.

Multi-office location businesses have a somewhat simpler task and need to examine whether they can reorganise in order to eliminate one or more locations by consolidation and improved systems.

Reducing revenue

The deliberate reduction in revenue can be a scary process for many managers, not just because it is antithetical to the precepts of most management theory which is based on a central objective of incremental growth. But also because managers tend to regard all marginal profit as being worth retaining.

So the important question managers must ask is, can a deliberate reduction in revenue be undertaken in a controlled way to facilitate a reduction in associated costs to leave the business better off?

There is nothing weak about deliberately reducing the scale of the company in order to find a more stable and durable base from which growth can resume when the climate is more favourable.

There is no rule that says worthwhile companies must grow continuously and, if they contract, it is a sign of managerial incompetence. It does not follow that because growth is associated with success retreat must be synonymous with failure.

Consider the military analogy. If an army cannot advance it may retreat to a more easily defended position, rest and re-supply and wait for another opportunity to move forward, possibly by a different route. History is replete with examples of success following retreat.

In a climate in which revenue is increasingly difficult to find it may seem paradoxical bordering on lunacy to inform customers that you will not supply them and thereby push them into the arms of your competitors.

But conducting a ruthlessly objective analysis of your revenue will reveal that not all customers are equally profitable, not all products contribute the same gross profit and not all regions are equally viable.

Shedding customers is always emotionally difficult for those who have strived long and hard to win business. The prospect of deliberately closing any account when the customer will probably move to a competitor is counterintuitive. Some would say demotivating.

So the way in which you communicate this move is critically important. Emphasise that this is the phase of profit not size and that it provides an opportunity to renegotiate existing customer contracts that have become unattractive because, if we cannot do so, we are no longer prepared to subsidise them to gain volume or market share.

Some customers may have greater prospects for profitable growth that could utilise existing capacity currently consumed by less profitable accounts.

In some industries the structure of the market may not allow the closing of the least profitable accounts.

A typical example is food retailing. Food retailers are notoriously tough negotiators who understand perfectly that their suppliers, the food manufacturers and especially those with secondary or tertiary brand positions, cannot afford not to be on their shelves with a significant presence.

So a food retailer will realise that access to its market share may determine the viability of the product and hence the manufacturer will be prepared to offer a better margin to secure a major retailer's acceptance.

Many people would regard this as a misuse of market power[22] and, if practiced unreasonably, it is prohibited under most competition law. However, it is not unlawful to maximise margins by capitalising on the leverage your position of relative strength gives you, and no buyer is under an obligation to purchase the goods or services offered.

Opening discussions with the least profitable customers about modifying the performance of their account by increasing prices or reducing the range of goods you sell to them by eliminating the least profitable products will never be easy.

If negotiations fail to improve the position and you understand the associated costs you are in a position to make a rational decision and you could cease to trade with these customers and explain to each customer why this step is necessary.

There is also something to be gained by giving your competitors your low margin business during turbulent times when growth in working capital is difficult and expensive to finance. It is unlikely that your rejected customer will move to your competitors on better terms than they were prepared to offer you.

In extreme cases you may find that your competitors cannot resist the opportunity to grow and that this is their Achilles heel that leads to their ultimate collapse and your erstwhile customers return to you but on better terms because you are a stable supplier. However, this is not an outcome on which you should rely.

I accept that deliberately reducing your customer base by closing accounts, abandoning territories and terminating products is not an easy decision. It requires careful analysis, good negotiating skills and the

---

[22] It is called monopsomy which is a market structured as many suppliers but a single or dominant buyer.

financial resources to fund the structural reorganisation necessary to eliminate the associated overheads.

Before you conduct the analysis of your active customers remember that you must also conduct negotiations with suppliers to ascertain the extent to which the possibility of reducing volume will cause them to increase the cost of material or components that you purchase.

As reluctant as you may be to refuse further orders from customers, consider if retreat over the short term means that you have a better chance of emerging from the turbulent times as a Healthy Survivor instead of a Disabled Survivor or worse.

Also remember that the action you take at this stage is about what you can and will become and not about what you are or have been. In the terms I have used earlier it is about 'becoming' and not about 'being'.

Defence planning

Your more enlightened customers will also approach you to negotiate better terms with the implied threat of moving their business elsewhere if you do not comply.

You must prepare a planned response to such approaches *before* they arise and not react to each as it happens. You should attempt to engage in these discussions in the context of a policy you have established for the business as a whole in order to avoid being drawn into a series of individual, uncoordinated negotiations.

It is often difficult to respond to a customer by saying that you are unable or unwilling to make any gesture to accommodate their request. In some cases it may be preferable to offer some price reduction or different credit terms to retain profitable customers. In more marginal cases this may provide an opportunity to inform them that their business is insufficiently profitable at the current prices and that if they are unable to continue on, at least, this basis then you may have to cease trading with them.

You must secure the perimeter of the position to which you plan to retrench so that your retreat into this secure enclave can halt at the point you wish and not become a disorderly rout as an uncontrolled loss of revenue reduces the company to an unviable size and shape.

Restructuring by abandoning products and services

A UK civil engineering and construction group, let's call it D, encountered liquidity problems as a result of its parent group stripping its cash to support an equipment leasing business that collapsed during a recession.

When construction companies encounter problems they tend to deteriorate rapidly as contracts are unfulfilled, actions are lodged against the company for liquidated damages incurred as a result of their non-performance, and new work cannot commence because insurance companies refuse to underwrite performance bonds in favour of clients to compensate for the costs of collapse.

Operating profits decline, prospects evaporate and the balance sheet is destroyed by the cost of litigation and the associated contingent liabilities.

If these problems occur during turbulent times then stabilising the company is made considerably more difficult and it is for these reasons that construction companies are often amongst the first to collapse during a recession.

An important feature of large construction contracts is that the project is cash rich at the outset but the cost of dealing with price increases, unexpected delays and unplanned work gradually imposes great pressure on the availability of funds.

The result is that sub-contractors whose work extends to the later phases of the project can find themselves under substantial pressure to reduce their prices and are not paid to time as project managers attempt to recover the cost of deviations from the original plan.

In the case of D the group's liquidity difficulties were made considerably worse by the value of invoices that were placed 'under query' and most of these related to late or end stage project activity.

I became executive chairman with a brief to stabilise the group as the principal bankers realised that the collapse of D's parent meant that in bankruptcy they would lose a significant fraction of their exposure.

The solution required a complicated reorganisation to separate D from claims arising from the bankruptcy of its parent and the urgency with which stability and financial security had to be re-established to avoid a terminal drain in confidence.

The action taken was as follows:

- On the basis of the plan outlined below lenders agreed to commit to a standstill agreement that stated that, unless there was a further materially adverse change to the condition of the business, they undertook for a period of 12 months not to take any action that would force D to file for bankruptcy or protection from creditors.

  Specifically this meant that lenders would maintain their existing levels of exposure and margin in return for a new schedule of covenants which provided them with an increased flow of information.

  Importantly, this allowed D to retain cash released from its 'receivables in dispute' balance and a proportion of certain disposals to fund its reorganisation.

- The standstill agreement provided reassurance to the insurance companies' bonding contracts convincing them to continue their exposure and thereby enabling D to commence contracts already won and to tender for new work.

- To release cash from the 'receivables in query' balance each invoice was credited and the work re-billed as an invoice covering that portion about which there was no dispute and a second invoice covering the amount in dispute.

A robust collection regime enabled substantial cash to be released.

- The decision was then taken to reposition the group by restructuring the balance of its constituent divisions so that D's subsequent activity exposed it only to activity that was completed during the first half of major contracts when the pressure on project cash flow was less.

This was accomplished by a combination of closures, disposals to third parties and divisional management.

The restructuring led to a contraction in the group's revenue and the loss of several long-standing customers.

- The outcome was that D had enough work to keep the restructured group cash positive for the forthcoming 3 years, by which time the recession was forecast to have passed, assuming only a rate of new tender success equal to the replacement of closing contracts.

- Within six months of the collapse of its parent D had been restructured and was subsequently refinanced by a private equity investor with the balance of the equity sold to a larger compatible business also funded by the same private equity fund.

Increasing margins

Turbulent times can imply a period of deflation when prices tend to fall as consumers and corporate purchasers attempt to reduce their costs by trying to reduce your prices.

On the one hand managers attempt to preserve or improve margins by resisting attempts by customers to negotiate additional discounts while, at the same time exerting pressure on their suppliers to offer improved terms of trade or moving to new suppliers in order to reduce prices.

This becomes a power play with the strongest being able to resist pressure from customers while being able to coerce suppliers.

But increasing margins is not only about bullying weaker customers and suppliers, it is also about being smart.

If increasing margins by 1% of revenue is expressed as a monetary value then, for a large business, it can seem to be a daunting target. For a company with revenue of 1bn and cost of goods sold of 50% of sales, consider for a moment which sounds the more intimidating:

- Reduce non-personnel expenditure by 10mm
- Reduce your purchasing budget by 2%

To ask each department to prepare a programme showing how non-personnel costs can be reduced by 2% of revenue and achieve this new level within the next six months is rarely answered by complaints of its impossibility.

To ask each supplier to reduce their price by 2% is rarely dismissed as impossible. It seems reasonable and manageable. Indeed, many will be expecting you to ask for substantially more so a small percentage is often agreed with relief.

Few people can argue against the following proposition that you might present:

> *Are you really going to present an argument that your operation is 100% efficient and that there is no capacity to improve efficiency by 4%, the benefit of which we share equally? Overall your business gains the 2% required and the additional 2% is an incentive offered to either employees or third parties who help to achieve the target.*

Speaking in percentages rather than values can make the task seem reasonable and more achievable.

Now, I am not suggesting that 2% is the target that should be set by every business. Many will require and feel able to demand larger savings. What I argue is that managers should express the targeted increase in margin in a way that makes it appear to be an achievable goal. Determine a small percentage that will make a significant difference to the company's gross profit but will be less than suppliers expect and difficult for both internal mangers and suppliers to argue is unachievable.

Also, by offering to work with a supplier to improve efficiency in that part of the value chain in which they operate by modifying your processes and sharing the benefit that results, converts the exercise from a zero sum negotiation into a cooperative effort for mutual benefit.

Additionally, you should ensure that, for major suppliers, each of your buyers understands how at least some of this saving can be achieved. For example, packaging redesign especially if you immediately unpack and discard this at goods inwards, agreeing to electronic billing with a quarterly account statement, identifying recent reductions in the supplier's input costs for raw materials, taking a full truck load every two weeks rather than half a load every week thereby halving transport costs.

Incentivising your staff to achieve the target by offering to share the benefit as a bonus not only motivates but creates a climate in which each person knows what they must do differently to respond to the turbulent times but shows that there is a measurable contribution they can make that is within their capacity and skill-set.

Involving staff in such a programme identifies for them a common enemy, 'cost', and sets an objective with measurable benefits that they can share. This is preferable to the practice of keeping the problem and its solution 'upstairs'. Employees appreciate that the times are turbulent and they fear silence about the company's position, often filling this void with negative speculation. They appreciate that they cannot contribute to and may not have the technical understanding of corporate finance issues but there are tasks that they can perform that have a meaningful impact, and increasing margins is one of the most important.

Prices

If your company has a business-to-business value chain you will come under pressure to reduce your prices at the same time that you are trying to manage your costs down.

So, if your customers adopt the process I've described above how can you improve margins at the sales end of the value chain?

Well, the truth is that the market is imperfect and many of your customers will not be as incisive or as inventive as you in managing the value chain. Those who are in denial about the impact that turbulent times may have on their business and those with high gross margins and large net margins will not resist a well presented case for modifying the trading relationship to the degree that others might.

The first task is to identify customers that are likely to be susceptible to a programme of margin improvement and formulate a bespoke proposition for each. Simply informing them that you intend to increase prices may work for some but for others it may cause a negative response that pollutes an otherwise good relationship in a way that you cannot decontaminate.

If you are able to propose to the customer a variation in the way in which they buy from you that would save '2x' on the basis that you share the benefit equally 'x each' then they will usually be delighted with you as a supplier as you have contributed to their profitability and, depending on the cost of the changes proposed, will usually regard the sharing of benefit as equitable.

The cost of cost reduction

Changes to business processes and cost reduction programmes such as downsizing are not cost free. They can be expensive in both actual costs of implementation but also in terms of disruption.

To manage this process you should evaluate the cost of each saving as you would an investment project. The list of projects should be arranged in order of their cash payback.

My usual methodology is to fit them into the following matrix:

Cash payback in	Cost	Ongoing annual cash benefit after payback
6 months		
6 < 12 months		
12 < 24 months		

Firstly, I want to ascertain how much of the programme can be self-financing and the minimum cash necessary to commence the first stage.

Secondly, I want to determine the net cash required to deliver the entire programme.

Actions that have a cash payback longer than 24 months should be avoided in the short term unless they leave only a small residual repayment. By small I mean that something like 90% of the payback is achieved within 24 months and the ongoing benefits are significant.

I then evaluate the programme as a combined cash flow mapped over a three to four year period.

Subsequently, I add the plan for the residual business and capital projects to give a cash flow and balance sheet picture of the restructured business.

Maintaining capital and development expenditure

The arguments in favour of maintaining capital expenditure and funding a full portfolio of development projects during turbulent times are weak. They are generally predicated on the assumption that stable times will return and a pause in product and asset development at this stage will leave the company disadvantaged when economic growth resumes.

Additionally, concerned employees, who can be emotionally invested in and attached to these projects, point to the sunk cost that may be lost by terminating a project at this stage.

There are two kinds of projects:

a.   Those already in progress.

b.   Those not yet started.

For both types you must revisit the original investment appraisal as the predictions about the cost of funds, the timing and size of inflows will all have been invalidated by the emergence of turbulence and, at an early stage, you cannot know the depth or duration of the storm.

Those already in progress

As part of the re-appraisal process you should determine the costs of premature termination and the capacity to re-activate and whether the associated costs render the project unviable.

There may be the difficult problem of having borrowed funds in the expectation of making repayment from the proceeds of one or more of these projects. The sum(s) anticipated may not be available unless the project(s) is completed to schedule and performs to expectation.

Moreover, the funds required to complete projects, which may be in the form of agreed bank facilities, may be withdrawn if lenders believe that the company as a whole cannot meet the performance and cash targets set previously.

If you confront this problem you must divide the company's plan into:

- A virtual entity consisting in the incomplete projects.

- The balance of the company.

As a crude beginning treat each division as a separate entity with no cross subsidy. Only when you establish the viability of each without the other can you begin to evaluate if and how they should be reconnected.

Each incomplete project must be evaluated on its merits but you have to formulate a plan that may involve terminating some (perhaps all), completing only those that are well advanced and using the proceeds to fund others that you delay in order to synchronise expenditure with resource availability.

Those not yet started

If these are not funded already it will probably be difficult to do so and you will probably need all the financial resource you can muster to fund the changes you need to make to the existing business.

The appraisal methodology should be consistent with that used in evaluating cost reductions so that the cash flows may be combined to give an overall picture.

The radical approach

In the spirit of embracing the unconventional and counterintuitive I can conceive of a business in which the current activity is reaching the end of its lifespan during a period of economic turbulence such that abandoning its development programme in order to preserve the current activity will lead to it emerging from the turbulent times as a dying business.

If the portfolio of incomplete development projects contains products that will replace those currently active but reaching the end of their lifespan the radical approach may be to dispose of the existing business and use the proceeds to fund completion of the development programme such that a new and viable business emerges from the turbulence.

This is not a solution for the faint-hearted but serves to illustrate that the decision about continuation or termination of development expenditure can be framed in a different way to the question how much can the business afford if the staple activity is to be preserved?

* * * *

In summary; what I hope you elicit from this discussion is that price changes without process changes are a blunt instrument and suggest, to whoever your counterparty is, that you are trying to pass your problem onto them.

The quality of presentation and detailed preparation are vital both internally and externally.

Remember that in turbulent times most companies are looking for good ideas to improve their stability and security, and most individuals want to be the bearer of positive news at a time when others seem only to report negative things. So if you can help your counterparties to achieve benefits while at the same time motivating your employees and improving your margins then the exercise is worthwhile.

It is important also not to rely on the achievement of a few big things but to recognise the holistic nature of the problems that arise in turbulent times. The big initiatives such as new capital raising or disposing of a substantial asset may alleviate the pressure on the company but, in turbulent times, these are uncertain transactions and take longer than at other times.

If you conclude that one of the big things, such as the completion of an asset sale, is achievable and that this will resolve all your problems that is excellent. But if you cannot deliver this then valuable time will have been lost and you are not simply no further forward but have also probably lost ground and credibility.

These big issues tend to be (indeed must be) few in number, non-operational and occupy the attention of a limited number of specialist people.

Operational initiatives must be instigated, not only to compensate for a failure to conclude one or more of the big things, but because they are beneficial in their own right and engage many people in a cooperative effort.

13

Changing the business model

Business models depend on the conditions in which they operate for their success. A model that has functioned effectively in stable times may be incapable of dealing with the changes that characterise turbulent times.

For example, a manufacturing operation that relies on economies of scale will experience problems if the market contracts or the distribution pipeline reduces inventories significantly and moves to an ordering pattern that demands small quantities delivered more frequently with much shorter lead times.

In turbulent times market pressure tends to push most businesses towards the need for greater flexibility and shorter response times. If business models are incapable of adapting then, just like species that are no longer suited to their environment, they run the risk of extinction.

Business models do not last forever and sometimes their appropriateness diminishes exponentially as new products and competitors emerge and economic conditions change.

IBM is a good example. A company which began in 1896 as a tabulating machine business with a business model directed towards business-to-business sales and servicing developed from the 1950's into the largest international provider of large mainframe computers, and changed again in 1981 to become a marketer of personal computers through a division that it sold to the Chinese company Lenovo in 2005. IBM now concentrates on providing IT solutions rather than simply selling hardware.

IBM has reinvented itself several times in order to survive structural changes to the markets it serves. As the lifespan of each business model has transcended maturity and entered decline, by radically altering its business model, IBM has managed to avoid, sometimes only just, becoming an extinct species because it was no longer adapted to its environment.

Changing a business model is like a biological entity rewriting its DNA to increase its fitness to survive in a changed environment for which it was maladapted. Turbulent times are the conditions in which this environmental change occurs too rapidly for some 'species' to adapt and their business model becomes dramatically non-viable. Some are flexible enough to modify their 'DNA' quickly. These are the Healthy Survivors.

Others can do so but delay doing so. These tend to be the Disabled Survivors.

Those that do not do so are either the fortunate few that I have called Resistant or the unfortunate few that either cannot or will not change and become Defenceless.

As I have stated elsewhere an important retrospective comment to avoid is:

> *By following the path they took to success... they eventually found failure.*

But changing the business model that has served the business well is a big decision and perceived by managers as a very big risk especially if turbulence prevails, as this is the time when their instinct for control inclines them to minimise changes and to become increasingly risk averse.

There is often the commonly shared belief, or perhaps hope, that turbulent times are just a pause in the smooth trend that has been enjoyed during the previous few years and it would be stupid to overreact to an aberration which is no more than a temporary interruption in the conditions in which we prospered with the current business model.

This is an understandable appraisal. Turbulent times usually prevail over a comparatively short timescale. This is in part because they consume the fuel of pessimistic sentiment that provides them with energy but they are, by definition, destructive phenomena, and it is rare that they dissipate without leaving behind widespread damage and even rarer for rebuilding in the calm following the storm to restore the previous environment precisely.

It takes very little imagination to understand that this is so. Consider the turbulence caused by natural phenomena such as earthquakes, forest fires, volcanic eruptions, tsunami, the Black Death, the two world wars of the 20th century, the asteroid that impacted 65 million years ago in the Yucatan peninsula.

Each of these events may have been of a short duration compared with the period between similar events in the same place, but afterwards the landscape, be it physical, biological, social or economic, was never the same as before. These events were discontinuities not pauses.

Managers who rest content that the turbulence will pass like a bad winter and that the economic spring will be like the last spring in which they functioned happily and successfully with this business model are probably deluding themselves.

The frost of an economic winter penetrates the fabric and exposes the structural weakness of businesses, damaging them to an extent that renders them unfit to operate with the agility they once considered necessary. So the business has to find another way to relate to the changed environment. It needs to modify its business model and occasionally find a new one.

There are two concepts that are in tension when turbulence reveals the inadequacy of the current business model:

1. The risk of changing a business model that has worked well and consumed substantial investment, to something that is untried and prepared for different conditions that, for the moment, are uncertain.

2. The risk of *not* changing the business model and finding that the health of the business deteriorates to a point at which greater change is required more urgently to prevent collapse.

It is the public healthcare dilemma of whether to invest in prevention of future disease or the cure of current illness.

During the turbulence you are unable to determine the future conditions with a degree of assurance sufficient to commit large-scale investment and therefore you must create greater organisational flexibility to enable the business to react adaptively to the turbulent forces at play and not to resist or try to divert the forces of change.

You must allow the existing business model to change even though you may be unsure of where the change is leading and therefore feel that you are abandoning organisation and control for corporate anarchy.

You must invest resources in continuously collecting information about what the outturn conditions may become as there comes a point in each turbulent event at which the aftermath becomes clear. This is the point at which you must decide the position you wish to occupy given the resources you have. By this stage you should become more risk tolerant and able to design and invest in a more robust business model.

You may regard this aspect as being too 'touchy feely' and want a more robust methodology. Well, so would we all, but complexity – and that is what turbulent times are, complexity operating at a chaotic frontier – has no statistically derivable outcome. Yes it may be possible to identify a range of possible outcomes by using techniques such as scenario planning but at root the process is qualitative not quantitative.

It may be useful to visualise this as warfare. In the Second World War, Germany and Japan each had a vision of the outcome in which they invested heavily. At the outset the Allies had no vision other than an abhorrence of the visions of the Axis powers. They had a simple general objective – to prevail – and that necessitated defeating the Axis powers by any means.

In the turmoil of conflict there was no clue as to the duration of the turbulence or the damage that would be caused in the cause of restoring stability. Determining the structure of the world that would emerge was impossible until, maybe, 1943, four years after the commencement of hostilities and two years before cessation.

The economic relations of the major industrial nations was decided in July 1944 at the Bretton Woods conference and the political shape of Europe was only determined in February 1945 at the Yalta conference, five and six years respectively after the commencement of hostilities in Europe.

In other words, 80% of the duration of the turbulence had to be endured before an attempt was made at shaping the post-turbulence world.

I suggest that this is not a bad yardstick for managers who encounter economic turbulence. A normal recession is 'V' shaped and lasts approximately two years from the start of the decent to the resumption of economic growth at around 3% pa. Therefore, applying the 80% rule suggests that you should not attempt to fix your business model for the next cycle until around 19 months following the start of the economic decline.

In the meantime you should release controls in order to create the maximum degree of flexibility within the existing business model.

But be cautious as not all turbulent events are 'V' shaped and neither are all recessions. The economic collapse that began in 1929 was shaped like a 'W'. Other recessions have been 'U' shaped and the Japanese economic turbulence that began in the 1990s was an elongated 'L' shape, mainly as a result of deflation.

The following chart shows the rate of growth on UK GDP. It illustrates the shape of the periods in which growth diminished and became negative and then returned to a positive rate.

It is clear from this why the 1970s have come to be known as the era of boom and bust and the unusually long period of sustained growth from the early 1990s until 2008 is visible.

UK GDP Growth 1970 to 2008

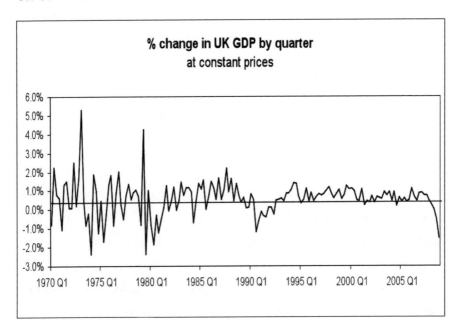

Source: ONS

UK GDP Growth 1980 to 2008

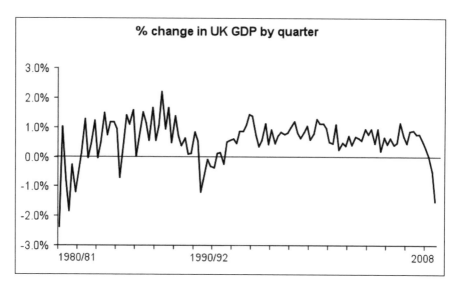

Source: ONS

The above figure shows the pattern of the last two UK recessions, 1980/81 & 1990/92. The first was much deeper than the second but both were predominantly 'V' shaped. I don't think the apparent 'W' in 1980/81 counts as a true 'W' as the middle spike did not arise as a result of growth returning to a positive. This arose in the US in 1979/83 and in the UK 1973/76.[23]

What is also clear is that for the cyclical pattern to have been preserved there should have been a recession in 2001/02 but, although the decline began in 2000, no contraction occurred.

However, it is also clear that, after 19 months of general economic turbulence, there should be some clues about the duration and shape of the recession sufficient to facilitate planning for the future.

---

[23] I believe that we must be cautious in looking at the shape of recession prior to 1980 as the structure of the UK economy has changed with the reduction of manufacturing's influence on GDP and, in the 1950s and 1960s the economy was still responding to the aftermath of World War II.

14

Planning for the future

Managers must assume that they face the short to medium term survival of the organisation in the expectation of a resumption in growth following the historical pattern of a 'V' shaped or 'U' shaped recession.

Most recessions are approximately symmetrical and while it is dangerous to presume that such symmetry is guaranteed, conclusions may be drawn from its absence.

Of course, the symmetry can only be perceived on the up-turn so the key pattern that managers must look for is whether the rate of decline is steeper or shallower than other 'V' shaped recessions. Coming out of a recession more slowly than the economy went into it suggests an 'L' shaped recession, most recently encountered by Japan in the 1990s when the growth phase was slow and hesitant.

If there is no resumption of growth within 12 months of the first quarter in which GDP contraction is reported then the presumption must be that the event is not a 'V' and is a different type that may take a longer period to resolve.

If this turbulent or depressed situation lasts for more than two consecutive years then a further set of conditions obtain in which the damage to the economic fabric from such a sustained period of distress is likely to be so profound that the structure of business activity may be significantly changed.

This is analogous to the effect the Black Death had on 14th century Europe in which at least one-third of the population perished. Afterwards, when the contagion ended, the society that existed before could not resume. The infrastructure had been disrupted, skills had been lost, labour was in short supply and at a premium, altering fundamentally the cost structure of agriculture and manufacturing.

During the plague the objective was coping and survival and no-one was able to anticipate the subsequent conditions because it was not possible to be certain how long the turbulence would last.

Our own turbulent times are, thankfully, different in type but are similar in character. In summary I set out below some of the key characteristics you should factor into your thoughts about the period following the phase of coping.

- From the charts presented in the previous chapter it is apparent that most general economic turbulent times tend to last for about 24 months.

- All turbulent times appear to conform to one of four basic shapes:

  V – assume 24 months from the start of decline to recovery to equal annual growth rate.

  U – assume 36 months from the start of decline to recovery to equal annual growth rate.

  W – assume two V's giving a total duration of 48 months.

  L – This shape tends to arise with the onset of deflation or the aftermath of an extended period of military conflict that destroys infrastructure.

  Considering each in turn will enable you to formulate a written sketch of the nature of the world that follows the end of turbulence and assess the condition your organisation will be in at this point.

- Some organisations, especially Disabled Survivors, may struggle with the after-effects of turbulent times for much longer. Many in this category survive as independent entities until phase III of the next credit cycle (see chapter 15) when they are consumed as acquisition activity maximises, fuelled by inexpensive and plentiful debt.

- So your planning structure should take account of the likely duration of the turbulence and within this horizon you must identify the best position you can achieve at the transition from phase IV to phase I of the credit cycle and plan the allocation of your resources to this objective.

- Your subsequent objectives thereafter will depend whether you exit the turbulent times as an unaffected organisation, a Healthy Survivor or a Disabled Survivor.

- The longer and deeper the period of turmoil the more likely you are to move from a Healthy Survivor to become a Disabled Survivor.

- The planning mode must change from 'being' to 'becoming'.

I suggest that the conventional financially-driven numerical planning systems can be misleading when undertaken from a position within a period of turbulence.

- You are unable to assess the timing or magnitude of demand recovery with an acceptable probability and therefore cannot construct detailed forecasts of the financial impact of the period following the end of the phase of turbulence.

- I recommend that the only valid basis for planning the longer term is to use scenario planning techniques[24] which commence by sketching the likely conditions that will prevail given alternative durations and shapes to the turbulence.

---

[24] See chapter 10.

The second stage of the planning process should be to add more numbers to the words to evaluate your capital and cash position and, given your estimated resources, the position you feel equipped to target in each of the outturn scenarios.

Your planning should have three components;

1. The objectives and actions to be taken in order to reach the final phase of the turbulent time.

2. The likely scenarios at the end of the period of turbulence.

3. The objectives, operational, financial and marketing plans for the three years following the end of turbulence.

15

The longer view

In the early stages of the business cycle managers plan for the longer term and see the short term as a period of development towards long-term goals. In maturity these long-term goals have been achieved and often people's horizons tend to shrink increasing to the shorter term. Sometimes a position of indecision is reached in which it seems inappropriate to set new long-term objectives because, intuitively, it is felt that the current trend cannot continue beyond the short term but preparation for turbulent times and the establishment of policy of preservation is thought to signal weakness. Hence the formulation of strategy in maturity is conceptually difficult and explains why so many managers enter turbulent times inadequately prepared with their resources deployed to support the accomplishment of unachievable objectives.

There are lessons to be learnt about the different ways managers should approach planning in the period before the turbulent phase of the business cycle, during the period of turbulence and for the new cycle that follows.

The conventional shape of plans is to construct a 5-year plan with the forthcoming 3-year period examined in greater detail than the subsequent two years. But it is rare for such plans to incorporate the credit cycle as an explicit component.

As we have discussed, economic downturn exposes the faults and vulnerabilities of economies, companies and business models.

The underlying driver of the business cycle is the credit cycle, which can be viewed simply as four seasons.

Season	Phase	Description	Asset prices
Spring	I	The period of economic recovery following a recession in which net lending increases.	Growing from a low base
Summer	II	The period of economic buoyancy in which interest rates begin to decline and covenants weaken.	Moderately high & accelerating
Autumn	III	Declining growth rate but lending growth and lending margin erosion continues.	Very high and still growing
Winter	IV	Recession in which loans fall into default and lending contracts.	Low

In a Western economy the credit cycle usually takes around 7 to 10 years but can be extended by fiscal intervention to defer much of the impact of one downturn. This occurred around 2000 when some degree of downturn was experienced due to the bursting of the dotcom bubble, but that didn't produce the systemic adjustment associated with a normal cyclical recession. The result was that the credit cycle never entered phase III until 2006/7 and the growth of lending continued to achieve unprecedented levels, especially in increasingly risky areas.

Few business planning formats pay sufficient attention to the credit cycle. Indeed, it may be argued that government, the financial sector and its regulators, that is those closest to the data, pay insufficient attention otherwise it is inconceivable that they would continue to run the system at such a high energy level.

It is analogous to driving a truck on a highway without exit roads, in fog, in an accelerating traffic flow towards a wall. Everyone knows that the wall is ahead but not the exact location and no one feels able to slow down because the traffic in front and behind continues to accelerate.

When the trucks at the front begin to hit the wall (the beginning of phase IV) there is a delay before the effect is felt by the following trucks, but by the time they hear the crashing there is no time to slow or take evasive action.

Why, you may ask, don't we recognise the conditions of phase III and take steps to slow the rate of lending growth to minimise the extent of the economic wreckage and shorten the time necessary to clear the highway?

The answer lies to a large degree in the psychology explained in chapter 4. Those who have prospered in the economic summer deny the change to autumn and, when they experience the early signs, tend to conceal them hoping that they can make suitable preparations for winter before anyone recognises their vulnerability.

If enough people behave similarly the collective delusion of a threshold is exceeded and phase III tends to be extended, adding weight to the assertion that the economy is under control and unlikely to enter into a downturn within the horizon of current plans and capital projects.

It is this horizon that is the key to planning for the future.

We may have learned important lessons from the downturn of 2008. They are:

1. Economic adjustments are necessary and healthy. Economies must not be permitted to miss a cyclical adjustment otherwise the unavoidable subsequent downturn will be greater than the sum of the recessions that have been avoided.

2. The international financial system is a global network and regulators must not be confined to making a myopic appraisal of risk confined to their domestic regime. As we have seen, the interconnectedness of the capital markets means that risk can be

located beyond the supervision of domestic regulators. A supra national financial regulation system is necessary.

3. Businesses that ignore the credit cycle in their planning must not receive new funds to fuel their reckless disregard of economic realities.

4. Governments must take greater account of the credit cycle. Of course, it is fiscally and politically unacceptable for them to pursue overt policies that presuppose the onset of a downturn as they control so much of the modern economy that their pessimism will be self-fulfilling. But they must plan fiscal policy over the cycle by recognising that funds for economic stimulus will be required at some point. So, when states receive repayment for loans made in the downturn of 2008 and a new cycle brings increased tax yield in phases II and III, governments must reduce debts in order to create capacity to borrow again in phase IV of the next cycle.

4. The political consequences of this are significant. The US holds presidential elections every four years. The UK must hold parliamentary elections no less frequently than every five years. A normal credit cycle last for seven to ten years and no political party wants to enter an election period at the time of recession and growing unemployment and so will attempt to manipulate fiscal policy to ensure that they can claim to the electorate that they have a record of caring for their economic well-being successfully. To this extent we are all economically vulnerable to political hubris and manipulation.

It may seem cynical to say that despite the harsh lessons of previous turbulent times we never seem to learn the lessons but that does seem to be the case.

Asset price bubbles are allowed to develop and are a strong signal of a subsequent period of economic turbulence. Lenders are allowed to use untested debt instruments to extend their activities into zones of leverage previously considered to be imprudent. Organic growth is insufficient and is supplemented and often replaced by merger and acquisition activity at inflated prices.

All of the above activities are necessary features of a vibrant economy and should not be prohibited. Nor can we or should we attempt to eradicate the cyclical turbulent times that are the result of risk taking. The adjustment is necessary and healthy. But the important lesson is not to allow these end stages of the credit cycle activities to operate for too long a period or for the cycle to be prolonged artificially so that the inevitable adjustment is more turbulent and disruptive than the sum of the recessions that would have been experienced had the natural cycle been allowed to continue.

16

Conclusion

Turbulent times are an unavoidable feature of interconnected market economies that occur periodically. Occasionally this cycle is punctuated by other significant events, that I have called HILPEs, that can knock economies out of their natural rhythm.

This pattern is apparent to anyone who studies the long-term movements of the major economies.

From time to time politicians claim to have eradicated the cycle. The long growth period in the Western economies until 2008 was such a time. The politicians were badly mistaken.

The reality is that there is something fundamental to market economies that causes them to behave cyclically. Econometricians find it difficult to isolate what this is and indeed it is unlikely that it is any single variable but a combination that interact benignly in one economic season only to become malignant in another.

My own view is that the credit cycle, which is easier to identify, the emergence of asset price bubbles and the psychology or sentiment of investors are, in combination, significant.

So managers will from time to time confront turbulent times but are not as well equipped to operate in these conditions as they are in the other phases of the corporate lifespan.

It may be that the degree of negative sentiment is a function of the length of time that has elapsed since the last cyclical downturn. If history teaches us that threatening events arise regularly then perhaps evolutionary psychology has programmed us to be alert to the increased possibility of danger if we have not felt the fear of loss for some time.

This is, of course, a controversial notion but, empirically, we seem to believe that the longer the period in which we are comfortable the more likely it is that some disturbance will occur sooner rather than later.

Turbulence, change and risk are related concepts that we have never lived without and have therefore come to expect that they will arise periodically in one of several forms.

Understanding what must and can be done to alleviate the problems that arise and to prepare an organisation for the different conditions that will prevail afterwards is not just necessary, because the turbulence cannot be avoided, but it is strategically important for organisational continuity and prosperity.

Considering turbulence from the point of view of the lifespan reveals that the turmoil that occurs during the transition from growth to maturity brings with it the necessary modification in the managerial mode from 'becoming' to 'being' which is psychologically different from that experienced in the change from maturity to decline.

General economic turbulence is similar to that experienced as an organisation moves into decline and in response managers must employ coping strategies that recognise close horizons and limited objectives. The strategy is to avoid slipping into the next phase of decline. But eventually coping must give way to preparation for a future resumption of stability.

This movement out of general turbulence has characteristics that require the management mode that is similar to that required in the growth phase. It is a new form of 'becoming' which demands a further revision to both psychology and the business model in order to establish a platform on which 'being' will again be the dominant mode with the objective of maximising returns. The strategy is no longer avoidance of the next phase but exploitation of the opportunities it offers.

While the lifespan concept provides a model of the natural phases in an organisation's existence the T-matrix offers a simple device for exploring the particular turbulent event being experienced and whether the principal drivers of turmoil are external conditions or internal discord.

Neither of these devices will provide generally applicable solutions to specific organisational problems but they will help you as a manager to frame the problem more objectively and to formulate some of the correct questions that you must answer if you are to cope.

Businesses that emerge from turbulent times with strength are better able to capitalise on the opportunities that arise. Indeed, I would go further and suggest that organisations that have business plans that are sufficiently flexible to absorb turbulence are likely to be those that deliver the best long-term returns to shareholders.

The ability to manage successfully or just to cope in turbulent times is an attribute that managers are well advised to add to their toolkit.

Appendix:

The Turbulence Matrix

The purpose of this appendix is to provide a brief insight into how to estimate an organisation's position on each of the axes of the T-matrix.

Axes of the T-matrix

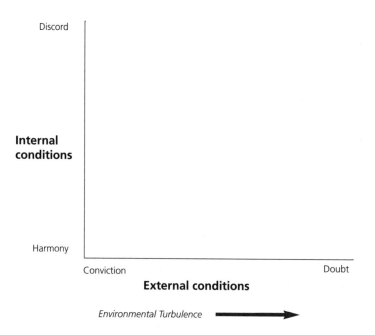

How to estimate the organisation's position on the vertical axis (Internal Conditions)

This axis maps the extent to which the management team agrees with the issues confronting the organisation and the decisions made.

The range is from complete agreement (Harmony) to strong factional disagreement (Discord).

I suggest that evaluation of the position of the organisation may be determined in one of two ways:

1. By asking each member of the management team to complete a short questionnaire.

2. By an independent observer such as an independent director or consultant making a subjective evaluation.

Questionnaire

I suggest that this should take the following form:

Determine, by agreement with the team, and list the 10 most important decisions taken over the preceding 12 months.

Ask each member of the team to complete a questionnaire anonymously that asks them to specify the degree to which they agreed or disagreed with each decision on the following 7 point scale:

- -3 = disagreed completely
- -2
- -1
- 0 = neither agreed nor disagreed
- +1
- +2
- +3 = agreed completely

- Add the scores and divide the scores by the number of team members and plot the result. -5 accords with maximum discord and +5 with maximum harmony.

- You can make the study slightly more sophisticated by asking each manager to weight each decision by its perceived significance to the organisation's future by placing them in rank order and assigning a weight of 10 to the most important.

- Or you can omit the aggregation and averaging stage and simply plot the average answers for each member of the team giving a spread of agreement/disagreement along the vertical axis.

- Or do both and show the average of all managers and the spread.

A significant difficulty with this methodology is that it is inconvenient to keep repeating the study in order to plot trends within short timescales. The practical solution is to conduct the initial study to establish a benchmark and then use the subjective method to estimate the direction of changes, and limit repetition of answering the questionnaire to a minimum of every 6 months when there are several new decisions to evaluate.

The objectivity of this method depends critically on the preservation of anonymity and you may wish to bring in an external party to conduct the study and prepare the analysis.

Subjective evaluation

This can only reasonably be undertaken by a disinterested party who is close enough to the management team to be able to form a balanced view of the way the debate about policy issues is changing.

A truly independent director may be able to fulfil this role or a senior HR professional should be well positioned to do so.

If the management team is beginning to become discordant and fragment into factions it is important that the person conducting the evaluation is not closely aligned with any of the contending groups and hence their conclusions cannot be contested or dismissed as prejudicial.

This methodology requires one or two individuals to meet monthly and discuss the atmosphere within the management team and to reach a conclusion as to whether the team has become more or less harmonious over the preceding period and to what degree.

There are clear indicators to be observed:

- If there is disunity does it result from the formations of factions that didn't exist previously or is it one or more people acting individually or is the CEO becoming isolated by colleagues withdrawing support?

- Is the disagreement about the conditions and problems being confronted with some denying they exist or are insignificant while others warn of their seriousness? Or is the divergence about the policies proposed to address commonly agreed problems?

- Is the disagreement beginning to move from healthy debate towards the inability to accept consensus or even threats of refusing to instigate policy proposals and suggestions by one faction that they will take the issue to the shareholders etc.?

- A weaker form of disunity that is often the initial manifestation of discontent is when individuals agree collectively to things that they disagree with privately.

In order to convert these subjective impressions into a measure that you can use to plot a position on the vertical axis of the T-matrix I suggest that, without consulting the previous measure, you decide how you would score the degree of harmony (+3) or discord (-3) with an inability to incline one way or the other as 0.

When scaling the axis remember that zero is not located in the zone of stability. I suggest that stability ends at a score of +2 or +1 with the origin being +3.

How to estimate the organisation's position on the horizontal axis (External Conditions)

This axis maps the management team's understanding of the external conditions in which the organisation must transact its business.

The range is from complete understanding of the causal relationships such that management's capacity to predict (with 95% accuracy) the conditions that will prevail over the next 12 months (conviction) to the inability to understand with any certainty (a confidence level of less than 50%) the conditions which lie ahead (doubt).

As with the vertical axis I suggest that evaluation of the position of the organisation may be determined in one of two ways:

1. By conducting a technical analysis using data that, in combination, indicates the degree of turbulence.

2. By employing a subjective assessment.

Technical

Turbulence is often described as volatility, which may be defined statistically as the coefficient of variation. Technical analysts of traded financial instruments have developed several mathematically based methods of measuring and comparing the volatilities inherent in markets and individual instruments.

However, the turbulence encountered by an organisation arises in one of two ways:

1. A HILPE. In these cases the event is readily identifiable and while there may be disagreement about how to respond there is usually accord about the source of the turbulence.

2. Volatility caused by the interaction of several variables each changing simultaneously and unpredictably.

The technical proposal I advocate relates to the second of these contexts and I suggest should take the following form:

- List not less than four and not more than eight of the key variables to which the organisation is most sensitive. For example, if you were a metal processor you may choose:

  - Energy prices on the futures market

  - The USD FX rate against a basket of currencies

  - The price on the futures market of the metal you process

  - The political risk in the region from which ore is extracted

  - The cost of a 12-month unsecured loan in USD

- You should then weight each of these variables in relation to others for the degree to which you are sensitive to each and place them in order of importance.

- You should settle on an external objective measure of each variable.

- Each month you should calculate the percentage change in each of the five variables.

- You should then plot the score multiplied by the weight you give to each variable on the following chart:

Turbulence Radar

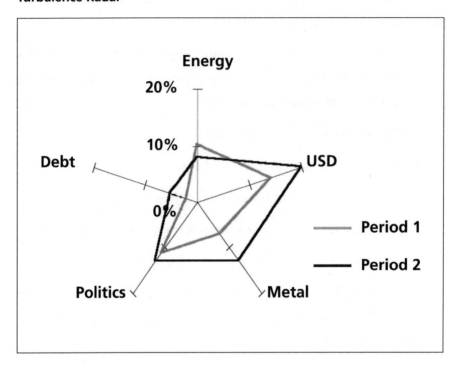

- This chart provides a visual presentation of the change in the level of turbulence from period to period and in the direction of the variable in which the greatest volatility is emerging.

- At the origin is the point of stability at which all the variables are at their values of least concern.

- In the preceding period you ask each member of your management team to provide their estimation of the change in each variable during the current period which you also plot this on the chart and by comparison with the actual variation you may conclude:

  - The extent to which management is in agreement about the changes and the degree to which they disagree.

  - The degree to which managers believe the external environment will change over the short term. Their anticipation of volatility.

- The extent to which managers are correct in their predictions and therefore the grasp they have over changes to the key variables to which the organisation is sensitive.

The final point is how to convert these data onto the line of the T-matrix. A simple way is to measure the area of each triangle formed on the radar chart (a spreadsheet will do this efficiently) and then compute the aggregate area (in other words the area of the polygon) and let the area be the scale of the horizontal axis of the T-matrix.

- The measure should either be the simple degree of turbulence given by the variables you select, or preferably,

- The variance in the area between management's estimate and the actual to indicate the degree to which management is able to make reliable predictions and therefore retains a good understanding of the external environment.

Subjective

This arguably more user friendly, but less objective, methodology relies on asking managers to answer a simple question each month as follows:

On the following scale how confident do you feel about predicting the market and economic conditions that most affect the business?

Very confident	+5
	+4
	+3
	+2
	+1
Neither confident nor uncertain	0
	-1
	-2
	-3
	-4
Very uncertain	-5

You can then take the average score and the spread of answers and plot them on the horizontal axis and visualise the degree of certainty and, by comparing the previous answers, the movement in terms of growing or diminishing certainty.

The origin is a score of +5 and the point at which the threshold of stability intersects the axis should, I suggest, be set at +2 or +3.

On this basis a 0,0 score would position the organisation in zone B but close to the threshold with C & D which should be set at -1, +1.

The threshold of zone E should be set at -4, -2.

Index

A

ABN Amro 140

Accident Group, The 185

adapt(ation) 6, 10, 22-23, 31-32, 191, 247-248

adaptability 16, 26, 105, 192

adversaries, nature and potential behaviour of 170

advisers 71, 86

Apple Corporation 140

Amulet Group, The 185

anarchy 56-57, 62

anxiety 48, 56-57, 65-66

Alverez & Marsal 92

arrears, accounts in 205-207

assets xvi, 6, 8, 36, 69, 75, 82-83, 89, 94, 109, 114, 199-200, 204, 244, 264

Atlee, Clement 144, 147

Automobile Association (AA) 185

avoidance 23, 25, 49, 151, 272

B

bad debt 118

balance sheet 75, 101-102

managing 199-215

Bank of America 112

Bank of England 213

bankruptcy 83, 89, 151, 167, 174

Barclays Bank 92, 112

Bear Sterns 90

becoming 33-36, 42-43, 49-51, 110, 192, 233, 259, 272

beginning 33-34, 49

being 33-36, 42-43, 49-51, 192, 233, 259, 272

Black Death 249, 257-258

Blackmore, Susan 126

blue sky phase 110

bondholders 74, 87

communication with 172, 174-177

bonuses 54, 239

brand 116, 171

Bretton Woods 251

Brown, Gordon 142

BSE 171

bubbles xvi, 6-7, 82, 264, 267, 271

budgeting 15

Bush, George W. 93

business

cycles 17, 158, 263

model 247-253, 272

D

Dawkins, Richard 127

decision-making 6, 27, 50, 94, 161

emotional influences 94, 112

opinions, obtaining others' 153-155

decline 32-34, 37, 39, 41, 272

mode 49

psychology 49

debt 103

debtors

dealing with 205-208

defence planning 233-236

Defenceless, the 100-101, 248

deferring wages 229

deflation 68

denial 43, 56-57, 63-65, 66, 95, 153, 161

development expenditure 222, 241-243

dialectics 72

Dickens, Charles 184

Disabled Survivors 100, 106-109, 192, 220, 233, 248, 258-259

discord 56-57, 62, 278-279, 281

disorder, reversion to 3-4

dividends 211

doing the right thing or doing things right 25-28

doubt 56-57, 62, 282

downsizing 184, 207, 219-244

Drucker, Peter 15-16

E

EBIT 103

economic

systems 5, 10, 23, 31, 42, 123

turbulence xv-xvi, 6-8, 11, 37, 102, 128, 258, 265-267, 272

employees 64

communicating with 181-187

Enron 7

expansion 41

external party, introduction of 57, 71-73, 142, 279

F

faction(alism) 48, 56-57, 62, 72, 79, 280

Federal Reserve 81-82

feedback systems 40

Financial Services Authority, see 'FSA'

G

H